Write
Well & Sell:

Greeting Cards

The Blueprint Series
Guides For Practical Writing

Write Well & Sell:

Greeting Cards

by
Sandra M. Louden

Marcia —
I've enjoyed having you in class — remember: the creativity will you nourish will become ideas that soon flourish.

Best,
Sandra Louden
7/7/00

Jam-Packed Press
Pittsburgh, PA

ISBN 1-892356-00-7

For Peter Mark Roget
"Who Says There Are No Heroes?"

THANK YOU

If I thanked everyone to whom I owe a debt of gratitude, the list would run longer than this book. However, here are a few I'd like to extend now.

To my family: Present and past—all of you. Every single one of you...especially you who have always given me the gift of time.
To my writer friends: We are something else, aren't we?
To my normal friends: Some new, some old, some rediscovered. *"I'm smiling as I write this."*
To my students, both "live" and "cyberspace": You never believe me, but I learn more from you than you do from me.
To the musicians: Well, you're always with me, aren't you?
To Brigitte & Bob: Your patience and ability to listen are unmatched.
And to Judy & Mary Jo: What a venture we ventured into!

Professional Colleagues:
Dawn Abraham who gives me nice messages on funny sticky notes.
Linda Auclair whose editorial help is always right on target.
Jonna Barry who bought my first caption a long time ago.
Joyceann Ditka who let me practice an awful lot of speeches.
Joanne Fink whose expertise and talent never cease to amaze me.
Liz Folger whose book got me moving again.
Donna Gephart whose e-mails are right up my alley.
Diane Gnipp who is a joy to work for.
Stephanie Grober. We always pick up right where we left off.
Joan Harpham who always shared her leads most generously.
Jim Hoffmann who is just a great guy.
Kirsten Holm who takes the time to listen.
Anne Kertz Kernion whose energy I'd love to clone.
Melody Martin who I miss. Where are you?
Stephen Morrill who is a great "CampusBoss" and mangrove swamper.
Michael Scheibach who appreciated my (quirky!) sense of humor.
Eva Shaw whose constant guidance and mentoring I can never repay.
A.J.Tierno who let me type what I wanted when I finished his work.

CONTENTS

Statement of Purpose   9

Part One: We Start!   13
    Introduction
    Occasions

Part Two: We Prepare!   38
    Guidelines, Market Lists, Need Lists
    Judging A Company By Its Guidelines
    It's My Office & I'll Scream If I Want To
    Files
    Supplies

Part Three: We Write!   63
    Dividing Captions
        Exercise
        Answers
    Thinking Broadly
        Exercise
        Answers
    Thinking Visually
        Exercise
        Answers
    Thinking Literally
        Exercise
        Answers
    Puns

The Ten Most Unwanted List
Expressions
    My List of 50
Initials
    My List of 40
Traditional Verse
Contemporary Prose

Part Four: We Sell!   111
    Submitting Work To An Editor
    Mistakes Beginners Make
    Why Ideas Don't Sell
    Writer's Block
    Your Very Best
    First Sale Syndrome

APPENDIX A: *Card Companies*   *125*
APPENDIX B: *Sources*   *128*
APPENDIX C: *Glossary*   *131*
APPENDIX D: *Wrap-Up*   *133*

This Blueprint Guide
VS
A "Regular" Book

A STATEMENT OF PURPOSE

Why should you buy a soft-cover, self-published book on greeting card writing when you can probably find a "regular", hard-bound volume from a traditional publisher on the same subject?

Good question. Let me answer it.

First, obviously, is the cost. You need only compare what this guide runs as opposed to a hard-cover book. It's less expensive. It's softer; it can be *thumbed through* easier, tucked in crevices as a take-along book. It's simply more *reader-accessible.* And why is reader-accessibility vital? Same reason people take a map along with them when they travel, rather than let it set on a shelf at home. You tend to *use* what's at your side.

Is this manual less valuable because it's self-published?

Well, you'll just have to decide that for yourself. I've been writing greeting card captions for over 14 years. I developed and currently teach a successful card writing course through Community College (Pittsburgh). Our State has rated my non-credit course "Occupational" instead of "Recreational," meaning the College, as well as the County, pick up part of the tuition tab.

Why? Because _my students sell._

Constantly. Consistently. Continuously.

When I started my freelance writing career in 1986, I knew no one in the business. I wasn't a former editor of any greeting card company. The only things I had going for me were a flair for words and the absolute conviction I would succeed. I was a stay-at-home Mom who desperately wanted to write and get paid for that writing while staying home with two small children. _I had no—let me repeat that—**NO** insider contacts at any company._ I wasn't even on a first-name basis with the clerk at the local card shop.

But my lack of connections didn't—_wouldn't_—stop me. In my first year of caption writing, I only sold three verses, but it was enough. Enough to tell me, _this is where I stand_. This is where I dig my heels in. This is where I write. I never looked back.

By 1991, I'd won the coveted _Louie Award_—our industry's equivalent of the Oscar™—and would be nominated again the following year. My greeting card work was shown on Live! With Regis and Kathie Lee. I wrote verses for people such as wildlife advocate/ actress Stefanie Powers and quarterback Bernie Kosar. I had my own column in our industry's official magazine, _Greetings Today_ I spoke at writer's conferences, conducted workshops, visited high schools and colleges on career day.

And yes, my book on the subject was sold to a New York publisher in 1992. It made it as far as the final galley stage and was about to be published when it was canceled due to a "shift in priorities."

Was I discouraged? You bet. Did I stop writing or sending out my work? No way. In fact, I became more determined to "conquer" the writing world. I expanded my skills, trying fiction, non-fiction, book reviews, quizzes. I was published in all of them.

Still, I always seemed to go back to greeting cards. Soon, I was introduced to the world of Cyberspace and instead of simply having students in the Western PA area—the entire country and yes, the world, became my classroom. I've taught on the World Wide Web since Spring, 1998 and have had students from as far away as New Zealand, Spain, Norway and Italy. Anyone who was interested in greeting card writing would always ask the same questions.

Have you written a book? If so, where can I buy it?

Going into this, my third printing, I have the utmost confidence you'll find this book packed with information. There is practical, nuts & bolts advice as well as writing theory. There are numerous exercises—designed to give you a portfolio of work, so when those first assignments come your way, you have a cushion upon which to fall. I've even debunked a few "sacred cow" theories—such as why "sending your very best" isn't always true and how the biggest scam—writer's block—is foisted only upon people *who don't write*.

And if all that weren't enough to convince you, perhaps this will. You have me.

Yes, if you don't understand something you read here, write me. Or e-mail. (You'll find both my cyberspace and snail mail addresses throughout the book.) I'll answer your questions, your concerns. I'll guide you over any rough spots, giving you the benefit of my experience.

Why? Because I've never forgotten what it's like *to begin*. It's exciting, yes; but also a little frightening. No one you know writes greeting cards. You want to talk about your dreams, your goals, but no one seems interested, or worse, they're skeptical, ready to push stumbling blocks in your way.

I'm here to move those stumbling blocks from your path, guiding you to write—and sell—your greeting card captions.

Together, we simply won't fail!

Part One
Get On Your Mark (We Start!)

Introduction

Welcome to the world of greeting card writing. Whenever I teach my 6-week greeting card course, lecture at workshops and conferences or simply tell people I write greeting cards, they generally ask me one of six questions (and sometimes all six!). So rather than have these same questions buzzing around in your head—when you should be concentrating on the real issue of *writing*—I'm going to deal with them briefly here.

I am constantly asked (Be Prepared! When folks find out you write greeting cards, you'll get the same questions put to you) the following:

- How did you get started?
- Where do you get your ideas?
- Do you draw the pictures or only supply the words?
- Do you work for Hallmark?
- Will companies steal my ideas? How do I know I haven't inadvertently stolen from someone else?
- How much money will I make?

How Did I Get Started?

I've already answered that briefly for you, but let me emphasize that when I began writing captions in 1986, time was a precious commodity. (It still is.) With two children under the age of 4, I had "snippets" of time; no more than 15 minutes at a stretch. Longer writing—stories, essays, articles—was out.

I was flipping through a mail order catalogue that carried greeting cards and noticed one of their lines. (A line is any group of cards carrying a central theme or look.) I also noticed some things about these cards that would eventually serve me well.

All the captions were very short; sometimes a sentence, often just a phrase. They were all *extremely* sender/recipient oriented, with a definite "me-to-you" quality. (*Me-to-you* is a term you'll often read in this book.)

These particular cards were all based on a pun or play-on-words. (There's a difference as we'll see later.) Some of the captions were divided into an outside/inside format; others carried the message entirely on the inside. There were some that depended upon a visual (picture—either drawn or photographed—in this case, drawn) to help get the message across; in others, the visual was a mere enhancement to the words. And finally, in this set of eight cards, all wished the recipient a Happy Birthday.

When it dawned on me this would be perfect writing for my limited time stretches, I sat down immediately and sent out a batch of ideas. (More on "batches later.) They all came winging back three weeks later, rejected, *but* with a handwritten note at the bottom: "Very close. Please feel free to try again." Within three months, I had my first sale and by the end of that year, I'd sold three captions for a total of $115.00. Wasn't very much, but it didn't matter. There were actually people out there willing to pay for what I'd written.

The first four years were the toughest and that's really what this book is all about. With the advice and tips I'll give you here, you'll be able to leapfrog over those years where I stumbled, made silly mistakes and often, just plain winged it. (I don't regret those four years, by the way; because of them, you'll be able to benefit.)

Today, even with varied credentials in such widely different genres as book reviewing, eulogies, fiction, non-fiction, quizzes and profile interviewing, greeting card writing retains a special place in my heart. The perfect potboiler, it's still one of the most "fun" genres around. (And we're going to discuss why that particular criterion—fun—is one of the most important in the business of writing.)

Where Do You Get Your Ideas?

Those of you who do other kinds of writing get this question all the time. And when I answer it for card writing by saying "anywhere and everywhere," I generally get collective sighs and eye rolling at what most people consider a generic, non-helpful reply.

So let's get into a few specifics. First of all, today's

humorous (and also serious, non-poetical) captions are a statement on life, not an exercise in joke writing or sappy *moon-June-spoon* type poetry. That's out— especially for freelancers.

Some universal themes today's cards touch on: Single parenting, dieting, men, getting older, paying bills, the environment, death of a pet, loss of a job. To paraphrase a famous commercial: These are not your mother's greeting cards anymore. Sources for these themes are wide and varied, including, but not limited to: talk shows, stand-up comedians, your kids, magazines, family anecdotes, statistics and plain, old eavesdropping.

Let me give you a few, quick examples. My family was being particularly demanding during one mealtime and I was popping up and down from the table like a yo-yo. Finally, out of sheer frustration, I quipped: "You know, guys, my main goal in life right now is just to sit down."

Ka Bam! Luckily I was about five years into card writing and recognized a natural line when I said it. I rushed to my desk, wrote it down and sold it the first time out for $60. When life hands you lemons...

Listen to children; your own and other people's. When my daughter was about 4, she and I were taking our vitamins...she, a Flintstones, while I had my plain orange one. "Gee Mom," said my Alexis, "I feel sorry for you. Your vitamins don't look like anyone."

Yes, you guessed it! $75 for a statement that

eventually read: O: (stands for outside line) *It's no fun getting older. Our hair thins, our waistlines thicken...* I: (Inside) *...and our vitamins don't look like Fred Flintstone anymore."*

Stories handed down in your family are natural cards. My grandma told me that, when, in Slovenia, she would see her mother walking down the street to visit, she would throw all her dirty dishes in the oven, so when Theresa came in the house, she wouldn't scold. The eventual caption? O: *Congratulations to the bride & groom! Now that you're into the domestic scene, you should know your oven has many uses. Baking...broiling...* I: *...stashing dirty dishes in when company's coming.*

You all have those types of stories and anecdotes in your own family. You just haven't thought about turning them into captions. And that's where my main job comes in. I can't tell you what to write; wouldn't presume to do so even if I could. But, I can teach you **how to think**; how successful, selling card writers **must** think in order to sell their work. And once you learn how to recognize a potential caption in everything that's said and done around you, you'll be 90% of the way to selling!

Do You Draw The Pictures Or Only Supply The Words?

Since the caliber of my drawing is stick-people and smiley sun faces, **I can unequivocally state, I do not draw and it has not hurt my sales.** (It's true there are a few—very few—companies that require the entire package—artwork and verse—to be submitted for consideration, but it's too small a factor to worry about.) In lieu of the actual artwork, however, the writer must describe the visual, especially for those captions where the words are not immediately clear on their own.

For example, a popular note card I wrote and sold contained the caption: *These days it's getting tougher and tougher to make ends meet!* Doesn't seem particularly funny standing alone, does it? But add the visual description I came up with: "Graphic shows woman exercising, trying to touch her toes, but not succeeding"—and the caption itself takes on a whole different meaning.

This process is known as Visual Thinking and we'll cover it later in this book.

Do You Work For Hallmark?

I work for independent agents at times, who may or may not eventually sell my work to Hallmark, but I don't directly send material there. Frankly, I never seemed to get around to it. I began my career with solid, mid-size companies that constantly gave me encouragement, feedback and most important, checks.

When I get this question in class, I ask my students to name some greeting card companies. I always hear Hallmark, American Greetings. Some give me Blue Mountain Arts or Recycled Paper Greetings; invariably, someone says "Shoebox," which is a best-selling line of Hallmark's. Generally after that, I get blank stares.

It's estimated there are between 900-1,200 greeting card companies in North America, which range from The Big Four (Hallmark, American Greetings, Gibson Greetings, Recycled Paper Greetings) to the "Mom & Pop" operations on the dining room table. But, in between both those extremes, are the wonderful mid-size companies—some of which take 100% of their captions from freelancers.

This is where I guide my students, because this is where they'll undoubtedly sell fastest. When they sell quickly, their enthusiasm surges and they're more likely to continue submitting. I've seen it work so often, I have complete confidence in my approach.

✔ Will Companies Steal My Ideas? How Do I Know I Haven't Accidentally Stolen From Others?

I really cringe when these two questions come up, because while they're certainly valid, there are no quick or easy answers to them. First, let me stress in my own career, the "companies stealing my ideas" factor has not been a problem. In my 14 years in this business, I've suspected it may be have occurred several times—very rarely, may I add—and my solution is never to deal with the company again, under any circumstances. These companies also don't appear in any literature I hand out. (One particular company was charging to read submissions; I brought that situation to the attention of Writer's Market, who does investigate such complaints.)

Most editors only have one major goal in *their* lives: to read freelance submissions and make a decision on them ASAP. They don't accumulate three piles on their desk; the work they plan to buy, the stuff they plan to reject and the captions they plan to steal. Just doesn't work like that. (Try flying a verbal idea to an honest editor. She'll immediately cut you off with: "Send it to me in writing. I can't listen to it on the phone.")

Look at it from an editor's point of view. How does she know the writer hasn't gone to the nearest card shop and "borrowed" several of the funniest ones to submit as original work? An editor knows what's out there basically, but can't possibly read every one of the thousands of captions published. It's a two-way street of trust and I've found most editors, by far, treat their writers fairly.

Which brings us to the second part of the question: How do you, the writer, know if you've inadvertently taken someone else's words as your own? Again, with the thousands of short captions out there, quite frankly, you don't. Basic themes—stress, family and dating life—all have similar observations and sometimes repeats do occur. (When an editor writes on a sticky note: "Have similar" referring to one of your captions she's rejected, she is **not** accusing you of plagiarism. She understands the "thousands of captions" syndrome. She's merely saying: "You are very close to what we buy here. Keep trying.")

This is admittedly a gray area, but I've always come

down on the side of, as long as the writer doesn't deliberately take another's words as her own, repeats can and do happen. At this point in your career, try not to be overly concerned with it; you'll eventually develop a sixth sense about what constitutes "too similar."

✐ *How Much Money Can I Make?*

This is everyone's favorite question and one I love answering because card writing is one of THE most lucrative genres around. It's the perfect potboiler (*writer speak* for "keeps the financial pot boiling" while you're working on other, longer projects) as well.

First, **don't** quit your day job. While card writing is lucrative, it's also sporadic and there have been periodic slumps in the freelance buying cycle through the years. Also your income—as in anything freelance—depends totally upon output. You're only paid according to what you send out; no extra cash just for trying.

Recently, I broke my own record—from $25/word (Yes, *per word*) to $33/word, which was immediately followed by $50/word. (For a two-word caption, I was paid $100.) I've never gotten a rate anywhere close to that, even from major magazines. In my own career, I've been paid as low as $15 for a standard humorous caption (luckily I know of NO ONE who pays that rate anymore) and as high as $150 for the same type caption. Sometimes, the serious contemporary prose (more on types of cards in the next section) comes in at a slightly lower rate. Also, the Blue Mountain Arts-type caption, which is so unique to the industry, is paid differently.

You probably won't get rich writing captions, but you'll have a heck of a good time. You'll be writing. You'll get paid for that writing. You'll be published and your words will be read across the entire country. You'll always get a pretty picture or photograph accompanying your words. Sometimes you'll even get a by-line.

Your words will be present at all the important rites of passage in life: birth, graduation, marriage, retirement, death. Your words are always there—congratulating, commemorating, commiserating—saying for others what they may be unwilling, or unable, to say for themselves. Remember, people may not always attend an event. They may not be able to afford a gift or flowers. But they will generally acknowledge most events with a greeting card.

Let's turn our attention to the greeting card industry itself for a minute. I'm not big on official statistics, but I'll throw three quick ones at you. Nearest estimates are that 7.4 BILLION cards are sold to Americans annually for a total of $5.6 BILLION. (This includes boxed sets.) That figures out to 235 greeting cards bought every second around the clock forever and always. (Or $217.21 spent per second.) The industry has risen every year—through good and bad times— since records were first kept in 1943, when sales were $11 million.

Personalize these statistics for a second. How many cards do you *personally* buy and send in a year, especially if you're a woman? (Women buy 95% of all cards; but from a writing standpoint, it doesn't matter your gender or age...if you can think "short and snappy," and understand the current "take" on life and its many situations, you will sell.)   Think of the unexpected occasions...a graduation, an engagement, a wedding, the birth of a baby, a retirement, a bon voyage, a hospital stay, a passing away. How about the impulse, "just because" card sent to a friend when she's going through a hard time? Or the hopelessly-funny card, purchased because of the shared memory it evokes?

Comparatively speaking, a card is not considered a major purchase (think about the cost of flowers) and therefore is bought without consideration of the price. That's excellent news for all of us connected to the industry.

Let's look at the actual types of greeting cards out there in today's marketplace. While such categorizations are always somewhat subjective, I've found four main types.

These are: Traditional, Contemporary Prose, Studio/ Humorous, Alternate.

Traditional

You've all seen, bought or received this style card. It generally consists of a *tag line* on the outside and rhymed, metered verse inside. (A tag line is a throwaway line: "Happy Birthday To My Darling Sister" or "For A Special Dad" are tag lines.) This verse is generally done in iambic pentameter, but not always.

This is not what card companies usually want from their freelancers. (For a more in-depth look at the misconception of greeting card writing = poetry, why not read my **Insider Report** for **POET'S MARKET 2000** , published by Writer's Digest Books?) First, many mid-size companies don't even publish serious poetry. (Note I said "serious." Humorous, silly poetry with a zany punch line is often in demand and I frequently sell this type of verse). The major companies that do carry the traditional stuff have either in-house staff writers to supply their needs or else a huge database full of poetry from years past, which they constantly recycle with new artwork slapped on the front.

Having said that, however, I will stress that if you write poetry, you must continue doing so. First, any type of writing is excellent practice and only enhances your ability in our craft. Second, there are mid-size companies that take poetry; in fact, I've seen the traditional stuff make a small, yet impressive, comeback in recent years.

Third, the greeting card industry is one that really does "live and breathe with the times." So, it wouldn't surprise me if down the road, a new company would crop up with, say, a name like, "Back To Basics" or "Nostalgia Network" and only take poetry. *Write what you like and what comes naturally.* Your writing will carry that intangible sparkle when you do.

NOTE: "Sparkle" equals sales.

Contemporary Prose

What I call *contemporary prose,* others term "conversational prose" or "soft social expression." Whatever you name it, this type of card incorporates soft, realistic writing that sounds as if a person is talking. It's generally non-rhyming and best thought of as a "vignette" of caring. Sometimes the entire work appears on the inside only; other times, the prose is divided. Often it's no more than a single sentence or even a short phrase.

Occasionally contemporary prose "looks like poetry" in the way the verse is set up, but upon closer inspection, you'll find there is no rhyme or definite meter. Dayspring Cards provides such an example:

O: *For My Very Special Friend* [Tag Line]
I: *Our friendship has been blessed*
            with trust and understanding.
        The thoughtful things you do and say...
                your concern through difficult moments...
                your caring heart which gives so much---
        these things have been such a blessing to me.
        THANK YOU FOR BEING A WONDERFUL
        FRIEND!

Contemporary prose is very much in demand from a freelancer's perspective. Although pay sometimes is lower than for the funny stuff, the writer who can consistently capture the intangible warmth this style brings to a greeting card will have more work than she can handle.

Studio or Humorous

Now you're in my territory. I love the funny stuff (editors love the funny stuff, too—it's where most freelance sales are generated!) and after over 14 years, I'm still as enthusiastic about writing it as ever. Those of us over 40 remember studio/funny cards around 1965. They were rectangular, ugly things with artwork resembling second grade drawings. They had shiny surfaces and were generally placed at the rear of the store. Nobody wanted to admit they sold such uncouth things.

That is, until those uncouth things started outselling their more staid, uptight cousins. Slowly their size—and their look—changed. They were downsized to the more conventional 5x7". The artwork became imaginative, beautiful. Photographed cards began springing up. Zany cards that carried a complete cartoon on the front with an appropriate greeting card sentiment inside made their debut as well.

The captions to these funny cards are cutting edge, timely, often sarcastic, sometimes risqué. They are not jokes. (You will see "joke" cards on the racks and yes, occasionally, you may even sell one; most freelance dollars, however, are paid for humorous, true statements on life.) When you listen to today's stand-up comedians, they don't have the same patter of vaudeville performers or early TV stars. Today's breed comment on life—its absurdities and foibles—in a way we can relate to and recognize. That same type of humor is the glue that holds today's funny cards together.

My **LOUIE Award-winning card** is a perfect example. Anyone who has children understands and can relate to the words immediately.

O: Visual shows Mom looking at her children asleep in the beds.
                    Caption: *If only I could think of them as sleeping...*
I: *...instead of recharging.* (© Current Inc.)

The following year, one of my captions was also nominated for a LOUIE. It, too, carried that element of identification.

O: *There are many reasons for you to get well. Your family loves you and needs you. Your family is worried about you...*
I: *...your family is totally unsupervised in the kitchen! Get Well Soon!* (© Current Inc.)

While I can count the silly joke or gag among my sales, they certainly make up less than 5%. Most sales are generated from those pithy, short quips that say so much about life—and by extension, ourselves.

Alternate
I loosely define the alternate card as those cards carrying themes which didn't exist (or barely existed) even 10-15 years ago. (Don't confuse alternate cards with alternate products. Alternate products are everything other than greeting cards that carries a caption; including, but not limited to, Post-It™ Notes, calendars, mugs, bookmarks, T-shirts, plaques,

beverage napkins, magnets, etc.)

The alternate-card category is the most fluid of the four; it really does flow with the times, exploring new themes and territories as they (literally) pop up in the news. The small or mid-size companies *always* break this new ground, taking the creative risks. (Another reason for us, as creative people, to reward them for their innovation and courage by buying their products.)

Alternate cards use *both contemporary prose and humor* (not poetry) in getting their message across. Themes here run the gamut—death of a pet, coping, single parenting, terminal illness, putting a loved one in a nursing home or hospice, quitting cigarettes, buying a new car, losing one's job, helping the environment, etc.

An excellent example is the Get Well card. Twenty years ago, there were Get Well cards. Period. Then along comes a virus like AIDS, where folks don't usually recover and the cheery "Get Well Soon" was sadly inappropriate. Newer, softer cards filled the niche.

An entire genre subset—that of Woman-To-Woman Friendship—also came into being around 15-20 years ago. This is the "just because" card and as writers, you should understand that this occasion (there are others as well) is an impulse buy. **No one goes into a card store intending to buy a Woman Friendship card (except maybe people like us!).** We go in looking for a Sister Birthday card and start picking up other cards at random, laugh out loud as we find the "perfect" caption for our friend Elaine in Cincinnati and literally, "have to buy it." (The "impulse-buy syndrome" is also a major factor in alternate products. As writers, we need to understand such concepts as "Impulse Buying" or "Rack Impact"—covered later—to produce captions that editors view as salable.)

An alternate mega-seller for Current Inc. shows a worn-out looking woman with a mop and pail. There are no words on the front and the inside simply comments: *And just where's that damn Fairy Godmother when you need her.*

One of my alternate verses for Renaissance Greeting Cards, Inc. was based on a visual of Cleopatra seated on her throne. Again, there was no caption on the outside and the inside carried the message: *Some days it's tough just getting off your asp.* (It helps to know just enough history to turn it into a caption!)

An example of an alternate card carrying a poignant, serious message is this lovely caption from It Takes Two.

O: *When we count our true friends we must not forget the animals, for one of these gentle companions may be the truest friend of all.*

I: *We are sorry to know you have lost a special pet.*

A long introduction, right? Yes, long, but necessary, for what you've learned so far sets the foundation for both the "nuts and bolts" of card writing, as well as the theory. Let's look at one last thing before getting into Chapter 1—that being the general cycle—an overview, if you like—of a freelance greeting card writer's life. Although this whole book is dedicated to that end, I find it helps if it's spelled out, briefly, in advance.

You start by knowing the types of cards (traditional, prose, etc.—we've   already covered that) and the occasions. (That's coming next.)   You then contact various companies by writing for guidelines and once those guidelines start arriving, you'll judge them with a discerning eye, to decide if your writing matches their editorial policy. (One of *the* most important sections in this book is how to judge a company by its guidelines.)

Between the time you write for guidelines and their arrival, you have some down time where you can sit back and relax. Right? WRONG! Forget down time; no such animal. We're going to get our supplies gathered and our office space in order, with some basic files to keep us organized.

Then, we're going to do some WRITING (Ye gads! Not THAT!) with plenty of theory and lots of exercises. Why?   When those guidelines come back and eventually, when specific assignments start rolling in, you'll have a wealth of captions from which to draw inspiration. When you have back-up "stuff," you'll be less likely to panic and experience what you *believe* is "writer's block."

Once we've got the theory down pat and the

guidelines in front of us, we're ready to send out ideas. We'll look at common mistakes many beginning writers make (so you won't!) and the most prevalent reasons why ideas don't sell. I'll give you my take on a few concepts, such as writer's block, sending out your very best and what you can expect after you make that first sale.

Following this, I've included some helpful appendices containing a targeted list of card companies to get you started immediately writing for guidelines. I've given you some sources for you to continue on your greeting card writing path, along with a compact glossary of terms for quick reference. Most of all, I'm always here, either as FelshamLdy@aol.com (just an e-mail away) or as **Sandra Louden, P.O. Box 9701, Pittsburgh, PA 15229**. (An enclosed SASE will aid me in replying). If you have questions or comments, feel inspired—or maybe discouraged—or even if you have an extra sample of your published greeting card work you'd like to share (I *love* getting copies of my students' work), contact me.

I was alone when I started writing greeting cards (Don't get out the violins; it was good for me.) You don't have to be.

And now, let's begin, shall we?

OCCASIONS

In most, if not all, genres, the writer is told to "know her market." In greeting card writing, this means knowing your occasions. You're all probably familiar with most of the occasions listed below, but you may not have seen them lumped together, nor have you really thought about them from a *writing* standpoint. (I will be stressing that throughout—you're not a consumer now, randomly choosing what you like. You're a writer, carefully selecting words *that will sell*!)

Knowing, understanding and defining occasions is basic to every greeting card writer's success. Keep these in mind the next time you visit a card display and see how many you can find.

I've listed the major category first, followed by the various sub-sets.

BIRTHDAY (#1 occasion needed most by all editors): General, Masculine, Feminine, Relative (Specific & Generic), Belated, Specific Age Mentioned (16, 21, multiples of 30 to 90), "Quinceanera" (Spanish for Young Woman's 15th Birthday), Mutual (Shared Birthday), Juvenile (Generally rhymed & done in-house), Birthday Wish From All (Workplace where many people sign).

FRIENDSHIP (Often listed as 2nd greatest need): Woman-to-Woman (Biggest increase in the past 20 years), Thinking Of You, Hi/Hello, Please Write, Sorry I Haven't Written, General Good Wish, Encouragement/Cheer, Lighthearted Cope, Serious Cope, Your Special Day (Worded generically to apply to many situations), Romantic Love, Universal Love, Miss You.

ANNIVERSARY: To The Couple, Husband From Wife, Parents From Child.

LIFE'S TRANSITIONS: Engagement, Wedding, Expecting (Parents-To-Be or Mom-To-Be), New Baby, Graduation, New Job, New Home, Travel, Retirement, General Congratulations (Specific reason **not** mentioned), Divorce.

SEASONAL: Valentine's Day (2nd Most Popular), St. Patrick's Day (Growing in Popularity), Easter (3rd Most Popular), Secretary's Day, Nurses' Day, Mother's Day (4th In Popularity), Father's Day, Graduation (Also Listed Under "Transitions"), Grandparent's Day, Sweetest Day, Boss's Day, Halloween (Tremendous growth in popularity), Thanksgiving, Christmas (#1 Seasonal), Hanukkah, Kwanzaa, New Year's. (Note New Year's is listed last because it's still considered a "Winter Seasonal." Valentine's Day begins what we term as "Spring Seasonal.")

GET WELL: General, Hospital, Operation, Get Well From All.

MISCELLANEOUS: Invitations (Birthday Parties, Seasonal & Transitional Parties such as Graduation, Retirement, Showers, etc.),   Thank You, Sorry, Send Money, Good-bye, Sympathy (Never humorous), Support (Let's talk, I'm there for you, etc.), Death Of A Pet, Loss Of A Job, New Car, Quit Smoking, etc.

Since the first three categories are fairly self-explanatory, let's turn to **Life's Transitions**. Transition implies change and while that change may not be unexpected, it is something out of the ordinary routine of our day-to-day living. We look to these changes as rites of passage—milestones—which we acknowledge by sending a card.

Someone you know gets engaged, then married. She gets a new job, graduates from college, buys a new home, takes a cruise. She has a baby—then another. (This is a *busy* woman!) Her marriage doesn't work out, so she gets a divorce and gets promoted several times as well. She retires and takes another cruise. And through it all, there's that greeting card from a friend—commemorating,   commiserating, congratulating!

Translating these transitions into sales requires that you, the writer, capture the subtle, different emotions that accompany these changes in the ordinary patterns of our lives. Getting married generally means joy mixed with hope for a future shared with another. Having a baby also brings joy shared with nervous anticipation of caring for a totally helpless human being. Divorce obviously brings pain and a sense of failure. A kind of Machiavellian revenge (like mixing Cream of Wheat™ in his laundry detergent before he moves out) may also be a factor.

Capturing these emotions, with words that thousands of people will see as being written specifically with them in mind, is an essential part of your job. As greeting card writers, we are the anonymous mirrors reflecting what others often feel, but are reticent to express.

Another category we should look at briefly is **Seasonals**. These are occasions which occur once a year, every year. Depending upon the size of the card company, they may publish one seasonal, all of them or none. The company's guidelines should tell you in detail which they handle and any pertinent reading schedule associated with submitting seasonals.

In general, card companies divide seasonals into two

main categories: Spring and Fall. Spring seasonals are more numerous and contain all the yearly holidays falling between February and August. (Note "graduation" is listed as a seasonal and also as a transition. Graduations themselves occur yearly, but not within every family every year.) Fall seasonals are the yearly holidays occurring between September and January, with Christmas being the Number One Card-Sending Seasonal.

We've already looked at specific examples of occasions that didn't exist 20 years ago when we looked at alternate cards. Not only have these expanded under the broad umbrella of Friendship and Miscellaneous, but under Seasonals as well. When I grew up, there were a few sing-songy, traditional poetry cards for Halloween, mostly geared toward children. Today, almost immediately after Labor Day, you can see black and orange sprouting up all over. St. Patrick's Day, once ethnically and religiously oriented, has transformed into a holiday when all of us add an *O'* to our names.

All indications point to a dramatic rise in masculine birthday cards, as well as cards that speak the *Generation X* lingo, with computers and on-line communication a hot theme. Any new trend or topic of conversation—often literally taken off the evening news—is fair game. All this is great for the freelance writer who can recognize a probable card-sending occasion and write the words to match.

Listing occasions, as I've done above, is a fairly objective, "by the book" exercise. **Defining** occasions is where your individual creativity comes into play, as the process is much more subjective. For you, the writer, to find occasions you understand and can comfortably write for, may take weeks, even months. If you're like most people, you have a natural affinity for some occasions and almost no feeling for others. Of course, the more card-sending occasions you can accurately and creatively define and write for, the more in demand your work will be and the more paychecks you'll receive.

Let's look at an example of accurately defining an occasion. You have an assignment to write Valentine and Mother's Day captions. You've let your hair down for Valentine's Day, pulled out all the stops and as you reread your copy, some of it even makes you blush. Now you turn to Mother's Day. You're still writing humor, but wait? Is it the same kind of teasing, playful, sexy humor you've just used so successfully for Valentine's Day? I hope not.

No matter how funny you might think it is, if you send that risqué Mother's Day caption to an editor, she'll flip it away and wonder what planet you're from. Picture your risqué Mother's Day caption on the rack. Sure, you'd pick it up, read it and you might even laugh. (Although I doubt it.) But would you buy it for your mother? Well, neither would the editor who's reading your copy. And neither would that 36-year-old average card buyer from Fargo—and who would blame her?

Quiz yourself right now. Which Seasonal lends itself to risqué humor better, Halloween or Christmas?

Which is the more whimsical Seasonal, St. Patrick's Day or Thanksgiving?   Which occasion would be funnier to talk about having "one foot in the grave"— 40th Birthday or Retirement?

We'll talk about common mistakes beginners make later in this book.   Some mistakes are purely organizational, such as sending too many ideas at one time. These are easy to correct. The more subtle concepts of defining occasions within acceptable boundaries and writing with an eye toward *salability* (which is how an editor views **every** caption she judges), are much more difficult and often the primary cause for work to be rejected.

Part Two
Get Ready (We Prepare!)

Guidelines, Market Lists, Need Lists

We've discussed the greeting card industry in general, the basic types of cards, the many different occasions published and the importance you, the writer, have in defining these occasions for the consumer.

Up to this point, you've been a passive reader. Well, guess what? The picnic's over and it's your turn to do some writing—not actual caption writing yet (although if you've already started, please don't stop!)—but writing to request guidelines from the companies that interest you. (Appendix A will give you some starter companies; Appendix B, where to look for more.)

You'll want to begin contacting companies you think publish the type of material you can comfortably write. What constitutes "comfort?" Only you can answer that. In my case, I don't like to write—or buy (remember the cards you choose for others often determines the style you prefer writing) the X-rated stuff, nor, on the other end, the highly religious or traditional verse. Neither suits my tastes and that alone tells me that trying to write that type of card would come across as stilted and therefore, unsalable.

⤭ Write the kind of card you buy and send! ⤭

How do you go about finding what sort of material a company publishes? Your first real exposure to any card company is through its **Writer's Guidelines/ Market List**. You can tell volumes about a company—a real case of "first impressions do count"—through what their guidelines contain.

So, what exactly are "guidelines," "market lists," and "needs lists?" **A set of guidelines** is simply what the name suggests; instructions from a company telling you what it looks for in ideas, the format in which it requires your material to be submitted and other pertinent information regarding the judgment, acceptance and payment for your work.

The **market list** is also self-explanatory; the types of occasions or themes the company "markets" and also any other alternate products it may manufacture, such as memo pads, key rings, calendars, etc. Many times the market list is included as an integral part of the guidelines. Other times it may be a separate sheet listing all the marketable items a company publishes.

A **needs list** is a list of captions the company *needs* at any given moment. (We don't mince words in this business.) It differs from the guidelines and market lists in that it contains *very specific information of what a company needs* **right now** and generally always has some sort of deadline date. Needs lists, while they may be included with the guidelines, usually are not.

Once a freelancer makes a sale to a company, her name is put on an active freelance list (if the company is at all organized) and as immediate, specific needs arise, she will be notified. While guidelines and market lists are generally professionally typed with some obvious forethought, needs lists are often hurriedly scrawled on a sheet of paper, sometimes in a hand-addressed envelope. When an editor's need for certain copy reaches the desperation point, the needs list can turn into a faxed, e-mailed—or even verbal—communication where the editor contacts her trusted writers with what she needs.

You will hear these terms used interchangeably and as in most things in life, the distinctions can and do blur. The important thing to remember is not to get all hung up in terminology;   all of these are basically blueprints to guide your writing into salable captions.

First Communication With A Company

Your first communication with a card company will be an informal request, in writing, for a set of guidelines. Once you've decided which companies interest you enough to request guidelines, (I suggest five to start) you're ready to write your letter. This doesn't have to be on traditional letter-size paper, although it should be typed if possible. I generally use a sheet of paper, approximately 6x9" and editors have told me they actually appreciate the smaller sheets of paper.

Your letter should read something like this:

> *Dear First and Last Name:*
> *My name is Sandra Louden and I'm interested in writing for your company. I saw your listing in wherever (or I saw your line of cards in a store recently) and think my writing style is compatible with what you publish. Please send me a copy of your writer's guidelines. I've enclosed an SASE for your convenience in replying. Thank you.*

If you've actually seen the card in a store and are writing based on your appreciation of the company's product, the back of the card will usually give you the name of the company and sometimes the address as well. If not, ask the manager of the shop to give you the location of the company.

In addition, if the company is average-size, it will generally publish different **lines**. These lines always carry a specific name and focus on a theme or subject around which the writing is built. The theme may be as general as "humor;" but often a line is more detailed than that. Again, the only way to discover all the exciting lines out there is by going to different card shops (as well as pet stores, boutiques, florists, gift shops, vacation resorts; most stores have a spinner or rack of greeting cards) and spending 20 minutes reading the racks. Naturally you'll look more professional if, in your request for guidelines, you're able to mention a specific line or two you've seen that the company publishes. The editor will know you've done your homework and were interested enough in her company—often more aptly described as her "baby"—to have taken the time to read her cards.

Always include a self-addressed, stamped envelope (SASE) in your request for guidelines. This should be a #10 or standard size business envelope going out to the editor as well as the one coming back to you.

Once you've written and mailed at least five letters requesting guidelines, your work has only begun. I'm going to warn you right now—don't get in the deadly habit of thinking you can sit back and relax because the ball is out of your court for awhile. You've initiated a communication with a business and now you must be prepared to follow through so that when the guidelines do start rolling in, you'll have material ready and waiting to send to your selected companies as quickly as possible.

During the two-to-three weeks it will take to receive the majority of guidelines, your work will be cut out for you. You'll constantly be scouting out card racks and spinners. You should also be observing the ages and types of people who gather around certain types of cards. Do the elderly go to the racks with the more traditional poetic cards, while younger people gravitate toward the funny, irreverent cards or is this just a stereotype?

Observe businesswomen and the cards they choose. Ask the clerk or store manager which cards sell best.

Store personnel are very helpful in pointing out which lines and even which specific cards within any given line are constantly reordered because of their popularity.

This is the kind of homework you must do during your "guidelines waiting" period.   Gather ideas, jot down potential captions, read what others have written. This isn't sneaky advice for you to plagiarize what's out there;   but, rather, an essential part of your research as a caption writer in discovering general themes that today's cards carry.

You should also be experimenting with your writing: are you more comfortable writing humor, soft prose or traditional   poetry?   Once   you   receive   various guidelines,   you'll   quickly   be   able   to   see   which companies   publish   the   kinds   of   captions   you've written.   Naturally,   those   are   the   companies   where you'll want to submit your work to first.

5-POINT, TIME-OUT CHECKLIST:
1. READ 2. STUDY
3. WRITE 4. WRITE
5. WRITE!

Judging A Company By Its Guidelines

If I had to choose one area in my career where I initially floundered most, it would be this one. I'd send for a company's set of guidelines and upon receiving it, would *always* send out a batch (and often many batches) of ideas no matter how vague, confusing or just plain awful those guidelines were.

I hate to throw in some bad news, but let's face it: there are card companies out there that are disorganized, with unclear and ill-defined policies regarding their freelance writers. Submitting your work to such companies will only waste your time and break your heart, as you wait weeks, even months, without a word regarding your submissions.

There is nothing—especially for a beginner—as discouraging or frustrating, as to have your work treated in so cavalier, indifferent, and yes, rude a manner. So how do you prevent this happening to your card ideas?

You'll always have to put up with some long waits and even some disagreeable treatment at times, but you can eliminate much of that by knowing what to look for in a company's guidelines. These should be look upon as its calling card where first impressions definitely do count.

A good set of writer's guidelines contains certain,

specific information. Here is my own list—one I've painstakingly developed over the years—based on personal experience. It is an ideal one, starting from the least important to the most vital. The first three points are "nice" to know...certainly helpful as background. The last four points are absolute non-negotiable information a freelance writer *deserves* to know.

- *When was the company established?*
- *What % of its published material is freelance written?*
- *How much freelance work does the company receive/buy annually?*
- *What occasions does the company publish & what is its timetable for reading these occasions, especially seasonals?*
- *Does the company pay **on acceptance** or **publication** of your work?*
- *Does the company give **specific examples** of what it publishes?*
- *What is the **specific payment** per caption?*

When Was The Company Established?

While this isn't a vital piece of information, it certainly helps to know if a company has had enough business savvy to have survived in an extremely competitive industry. My rule of thumb is not to deal with companies less than two years old as they tend to be disorganized in their freelance policies.

For example, I once received a wonderful set of

guidelines from a brand new company explaining in detail all the occasions they were publishing. After I'd submitted several batches of work covering these occasions, I received another letter telling me they were sorry, but now they only published Birthday and Friendship because the other categories "just weren't selling." All those card ideas I'd submitted for everything other than Birthday and Friendship never stood a chance from the get go.

My own theory on new card companies is they are often started by people who have the idea it would be *fun* to make cards; these people often being frustrated writers, artists or photographers. Once they start the company, they quickly find out the challenge isn't *creating* a line of cards, but rather, *marketing* them in an already crowded arena and *selling* them to the consumer who has thousands of other cards from which to choose. There are still many "niches" out there waiting for an innovative card company to fill; unfortunately, many new companies run out of money, time and patience before they find that niche.

You, the writer, waiting by your mailbox for this promising new company to buy all your ideas, get caught in the squeeze. You'll want to be flexible and if a new company seems especially well-organized and publishes unique cards, try them. In general, however, stick with companies that have a proven track record, have been through several seasons of card-sending occasions and have a firm grip on what they want to publish and what is actually salable.

✔ What Percent Of The Company's Published Material Is Freelance Written?

✔ How Much Do They Receive/Buy?

I list these two together because they are really flip sides of the same coin. Again, this information is not essential, but it certainly helps you get a handle on what you're up against as far as competition either from other freelance writers, or in the case of a large company, their own in-house staff of writers.

Out of all the criteria you should use to judge a company, this is the most flexible. There are dozens of mix-and-match patterns. A company, for instance, may only purchase 10% of its line from freelance writers; however, if this is paired with the fact that the company receives just 150 submissions annually (and produces a kind of card that is right up your alley writing-wise), it may be worth your time and effort to work for this company.

✔ What Occasions Do They Publish & How Quickly Do They Read Them?

Smaller companies may only publish the basic non-seasonals—Birthday, General Friendship, Anniversary and Get Well, with no seasonal holidays at all. Other small companies may only publish a Christmas, Valentine, and Mother's Day line of seasonals. Mid-size or large companies will publish all the above occasions and a myriad of other combinations ranging from St. Patrick's Day and Kwanzaa to the more unusual alternate lines of travel, divorce or new car.

The point here is, the guidelines must tell you what occasions are published, so you don't waste your time submitting what they won't even consider. Also, besides telling you what their published occasions are, the company should set forth a definite timetable for submitting these ideas.

Most companies look at any ideas all year long (with specific needs occurring when they...*need* them) which, of course, is easiest for the writer. Some, however, have a set time frame, especially for the judging of Seasonal ideas. This time frame is usually set up in a 6, 12 or 18 month cycle. This simply means if they want Seasonals submitted 6 or 18 months in advance (it's the same schedule), you must flip-flop your thinking so you can send out your Fall stuff in the Spring and vice versa. A 12-month schedule is just that; send your Fall ideas in the Fall, Spring in the Spring.

There are still other companies that will tell you to submit material from, say, January through May. After May, they stop looking at any new submissions and begin judging what has come in since January. This is my least favorite kind of timetable because not only does it mean that for seven months out of the year, a writer can't submit any new ideas, it also means any idea you've sent won't even be looked at or judged until after May 31st. That's a long, inconvenient wait for the writer.

My point here, however, is not **what** the timetable is,

but rather that the company spell it out beforehand, accurately and in detail. You then have the option of deciding whether the company's schedule for submitting ideas suits your work habits.

Do Companies Pay On Acceptance Or Publication Of Your Work?

This is an extremely important point for the freelance writer and one which a novice often overlooks because he doesn't understand the full ramifications of each policy.

Let's set up two scenarios. In the first, the company pays on acceptance. This means the editor will look at your work, make a decision as to what she'll buy and then inform you what she has accepted **with payment enclosed**. This decision process may be as short as four weeks or as long as several months. (Once again, the guidelines should give you at least a rough estimate of how long the judging process takes.)

Nevertheless, once your material has been accepted, you, the writer, **are paid**. The sentiment no longer belongs to you; your signature on the back of the check (or on a waiver the company will send you) signifies you've turned over all rights for the work to the company. Your end of the bargain has been fulfilled; you have written a good piece of copy and have been rewarded monetarily for your efforts. You're free to move on to other ideas. Neat. Cut and dry. Case closed.

In the second scenario, the company pays on publication. Here, you send in your material and within the same time constraints as above, you're advised by the editor that she's "holding" your idea or even that she has "accepted" your idea. However, since the company only pays when it publishes your sentiment, **there is no check enclosed** with the editor's decision. The company has subtly turned the tables against you because they have "accepted" your idea (which by implication means you can't send it to anyone else), but have not had to pay for it.

When will the company publish it? Might be a month, might be 14 years. (The first caption I ever sold still hasn't been published.) Remember, we're talking about a piece of work that generally doesn't run over 20 words. It's enough of a negative that we've sold all rights to the work; I view it as adding insult to injury by then, only receiving pay when the work is published, rather than when it has been accepted.

Here, though, is an excellent time to make a valid point. **The captions you write are your material and you are responsible for them**. If after four months, you've received no word from the company regarding your held ideas, you should write or call, inquiring about the status of your work. Sometimes that nudge is enough to have an editor make a decision.

If not, you have two options. Either tell the editor you want to be free to send the work to other companies, even while she's "holding" your work, and if another editor sends you a check first, you'll immediately advise her someone else has bought it.   If the first editor nixes this suggestion, then you, the writer, must decide how long you're willing to let her "hold" your work without receiving compensation.

✔ Do Companies Give Examples Of The Captions They Publish?

This point is particularly relevant for mid-size or smaller companies whose cards may not be readily available for inspection at the local mall. Whether the company includes these examples as part of their standard set of guidelines or whether it provides, for a small fee, a separate brochure for the freelancer, it's essential the company shows its prospective writers exactly the kind of material it publishes. A generic statement like: "We publish humorous, *me-to-you* cards" just wastes everyone's time. Every card has (or should have) a *me-to-you* message; that's the sole function in life for a greeting card.

As you've probably already noticed as well, *humorous* runs the gamut from soft, cuddly G-rated to the *get down*, four-letter word, X-rated stuff. In between "G" and "X," there's a whole world of funny stuff. By seeing the kinds of cards a company publishes (or even just by reading some of the captions which have been typed in the guidelines), you'll know immediately if this is what you want to write. You won't waste your time, or an editor's, by sending material which is well-written and professional, but simply "wrong" for the company.

Do The Guidelines Give Specific Payment Rates For Captions?

You'd think this would be a basic component in any set of guidelines, wouldn't you? Surprisingly, it often is not. Some companies don't put forth any payment rate in their guidelines; opting instead for statements such as: "We pay according to industry standards," "Our rates are competitive to the industry," or "The amount varies with how much editing is required to make the caption appropriate."

Can we talk? "Freelance" is defined in Webster's as: "A writer, actor, etc. who is not under contract for regular work but sells his [sic] writings or services to individual buyers." In other words, as freelancers, we receive no fringe benefits from a company—no vacation pay, no insurance, no pension, not even a Christmas party. Quite frankly, the dollar amount is what it's all about.

In fairness to companies that seem evasive about pay rates, I don't think it necessarily shows dishonesty or lack of good faith on their part. I've found, however, it can show a lack of organization and a distinct unwillingness to commit themselves to a fee. "Industry standards" today vary from $25 to $175 for a single caption; we're talking a wide playing field here. "Competitive to the industry" is no better—what the company sees as competitive, compared to the writer's view, will almost certainly be two entirely different amounts. Paying according to "how much editing is required" is nebulous. What is the going rate today for adding a "the," subtracting an "of," or changing an "I" to a "we?"

Of all the criteria I've given for judging a company by its guidelines, this is obviously the most important. You'd never start a "traditional" 8-5 job without knowing your salary; you shouldn't do it here either.

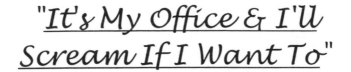

"It's My Office & I'll Scream If I Want To"

Before you sit down to create those fabulous ideas, you'll have to decide **where** you're going to sit. It's been said (I'm the one who said it) that the ideal office in any room with a door and a lock. It doesn't have to be the size of a football stadium; even a walk-in closet space is okay as long as you can retreat into it and shut the rest of the world out. ("Rest of the world" is a euphemism for "your family." More on them soon.)

Remember, I said *ideal* and in this less-than-perfect world, I still haven't attained the "door and lock" thing. I mention this not to complain, but rather to make the point that most people don't have that extra spare room in their house or apartment that can be magically turned into an exclusive office. It's nice if you do; but not disastrous if you don't.

What **is** imperative, however, is having some space—any space, no matter how tiny—that is yours and yours alone. Preferably this area should be out of the way of the family's traffic patterns. A corner of the bedroom or a section of your laundry room—anywhere you can carve out a section that won't disrupt the flow of everyday life.

Where your new office is situated isn't as important as constantly keeping it in the same place! Creating captions will quickly become a chore if every time you sit down, you first have to clear the dining room table, set up your supplies and reference materials—all the while keeping an eye on the clock so you can once again get the table back to its original state in time for dinner. If you only have 30 minutes daily to create and type your ideas, you don't want to spend 20 minutes of that time preparing to do so.

Deciding where your office will be located is only half the challenge. The other half is getting your family to accept your office for what it is—your professional work space that, coincidentally, just happens to be located within your home.

Fortunately, today, home offices are *in* like never before.   When you work from your home, you've attained what many see as the ideal life; also, if statistics are to be believed, home office workers are rapidly becoming the norm, rather than the exception. Your new employment status probably will be accepted without too much ado.

It wasn't that way when I started writing cards; in fact, I overcame some major hurdles in attitude—not only my own, but from people around me. I was told mine wasn't a "regular" job and wasn't it nice I was earning "pin money" (yes, "pin money"—a term I'd thought had gone out with corsets) and "keeping busy." I once called a business office that had sent me an incorrect earnings form, only to be told: "What office machines could you possibly have?". Well-meaning friends and relatives, who wouldn't have dreamed of phoning or "stopping by" at a traditional place of employment, phoned. Stopped by.

In the beginning, I may have subtly encouraged this behavior because I hadn't yet developed the discipline and single-mindedness required to work at home. I soon learned, however, as you will, to set up a few common sense rules.

First, establish a specific work time each day and then, during that time, **WORK!** It doesn't matter if you only have 20 minutes a day to write; in fact, that's about what I had when I began my career. The important thing is to make your allotted writing time become as much a part of your daily routine as brushing your teeth or washing your face. You know how you feel if you skip those hygienic rituals; well, you should have that same feeling if you miss your wordsmith session.

During this time, don't answer the door or the phone. (Put the answering machine on and don't be tempted to pick up the receiver). Work around your children's natural napping time, or if they're older, their school day. Even when they're playing around you, develop the habit of always carrying a notebook and pen to jot down ideas for captions as they occur to you.

As your children get older, you'll find you're up against another type of challenge in the constant struggle to keep your office intact and self-contained. As they become more aware of what you do, they'll be fascinated and proud of your work, particularly when they see one of *your* verses in an actual card. Funny cards, especially, often have an animated, cartoon look that children love.

Your work, in fact, may seem like so much fun that your children will pay you the highest compliment by wanting to have a home office of their own. That's fine—as far as it goes. However, your office should not become a wellspring of paper clips, tape, staples, pens or postage stamps, for everyone's private use. (Postage stamps are brightly colored and can stick **anywhere**; keep them hidden in a drawer!) You'll feel like the Wicked Witch of the West at first—nit-picking about who used half-a-roll of tape or let the cap off your highlighter—but it really is vital your family understands and respects that your success depends in large part on having an area that's considered yours alone; a place not to be touched without your permission.

It's been said a worker is only as good as her tools. That applies to a writer, her office and supplies, as well.

Files

Fortunately, filing isn't a major factor in this business, but there are a few files you'll need to keep and refer to with varying frequency. If possible, you'll want a hanging file-folder system; it's much more efficient because you can see the tabs at a glance without them "slouching" together.

Below are my suggestions for files, followed by a brief description of each.

Submissions File

This is your back-up file; your copy of ideas sent out to an editor (Remember: **NEVER, EVER** send your only copy of anything!) and one you'll find yourself referring to constantly. With the advent of computers and e-mail submissions, your submissions file may end up being stored on your hard drive or a floppy disk. Whatever form—traditional paper or electronic—it should be accurate and intact before your original work leaves on its way to an editor.

Guidelines File

As we've already discussed, guidelines are the blueprints from a company that direct the writer. You'll want to file your guidelines, referring to them often before sending ideas to an editor. Even after you've formed a successful relationship with a company, you'll want to request a revised set of guidelines every few years to keep this file current.

Needs File

Once you begin selling, companies will send you brief notices of what they need, often with a definite deadline date included. If you don't have a hanging bulletin board where you can post these notices for easy reference, the next best thing is to keep a separate file marked: *Current Needs.* Naturally, you'll refer to this file often, so as not to let a deadline date slide by unnoticed. This will be your most "fluid" file; you'll replace needs lists often, as a company updates them or as their deadline dates expire.

Acceptance File

In my personal files, acceptances take on two forms. One is the hanging file in which the actual acceptance letters or contracts are stored. To the backs of these letters/contracts, I staple the check stub. The second acceptance file is a box, with alphabetical dividers, that holds 3x5" cards with the sold captions typed on them. Under the caption, I type relevant information on where the caption was sold, the date sold and how much I was paid.

Rejection File

This is the file that keeps you humble. It also provides easy reference for those captions that were "held" but for whatever reason, didn't sell. You'll definitely want to keep these "almost made it" captions separate from the general rejects. Eventually with a little reworking (or sometimes no reworking at all...just submitting to another company), you can turn these "almosts" into a sale.

Ideas File

Your "ideas" file should be an informal, *user-friendly* file full of possible ideas for captions you've run across in magazines, newspapers or even heard (or *overheard*) in conversations. With this file within easy reach, you'll never forget or lose any ideas that eventually could be turned into cash.

Visual File

Just as the name suggests, your visual file will contain

pictures you've seen that "say it all." These visuals should come from a variety of sources and you should consciously spend time expanding this file as it will be an excellent source when it comes time for those brainstorming sessions. Even more so than when I started in 1986, greeting cards rely on strong visuals—photographs are increasingly popular—to get the message across. Besides that, both your ideas and visual files are the "fun files" that will keep you motivated, even on days when you feel your creativity is tapped out entirely.

Supplies

The good news—no, let me rephrase that—the *great* news about supplies is your overhead as a freelance caption writer is extremely low. It's helpful to have a computer or typewriter—the latter with a correcting key to save time—but if you don't, it's no big deal. Editors do accept work printed neatly in pen.

That's the extent of modern technology, since I assume you have a phone to talk to editors should the need arise. After that you'll need the following:

- 3x5" white, unlined index cards (At least 500)
- Rubber stamp with name, address and phone
- Ink pad (for the rubber stamp)
- Notebook for jotting down ideas
- #10, business-size envelopes (at least 100)
- Roll of first class postage stamps
- Reference books such as dictionary, thesaurus (Hats off to Peter Mark Roget here!) and any quotation books
- Standard office equipment including pens, rubber bands, paper clips, stapler, small calendar to note deadlines, etc.

You probably have most, if not all these supplies already scattered around the house. The trick is to gather them all together in one place, designate that place an office and gently, but firmly and consistently, insist that this place be respected as your working area.   Laying these ground rules early will prevent later misunderstanding and frustration.   Having a stationary area that is yours alone (especially in a house or apartment where you laboriously have *to carve that space out* for yourself) will also put subtle pressure on you to continue working daily to justify having that space.

PART THREE
GET SET (WE WRITE!)

Dividing Captions

In the days before contemporary, humorous cards became popular, dividing a caption was unnecessary. There was a tag line (sometimes also referred to as a "cover headline") on the outside and a complete, traditional verse on the inside. Today, however, most humorous greeting cards (and some contemporary prose) have an outside/inside format, in which the outside caption "sets up" or hooks the reader; she expects a certain completion or ending of the thought begun on the outside and is then fooled by how the inside line reads.

For maximum comedic (or poignant) effect, the caption must be divided correctly, giving the best spin to the words without giving away the punch line on the inside. Sometime the best division is no division at all; the best effect would be to read all the words together on the inside, letting the picture on the outside do all the initial "sales" work.

It's up to you, the writer, to decide where—or whether—the caption should be divided. Through practice, you'll learn which words "hook" and how they manage to do so. The exercise following this section will get you started.

Another consideration that goes right along with dividing a caption is determining when and how often you should mention the specific occasion for which the caption is written. Walk into any card shop and notice how the cards are arranged. If they're part of a spinner, you can generally see most the card's surface.

However, the more common display today is for the cards to be tiered in a rack, with only the top third of the card visible to the eye. This means that only the first and possibly second line of the caption are visible until the consumer actually picks up the card to read it. (As a writer, you should also know that each card has a second-and-a-half to catch the consumer's eye before she moves on to the next. This is known as **rack impact**—a concept *every* editor keeps in mind when she considers a writer's work!)

You've all picked up a card where you weren't sure what the occasion was until you read the inside. That's not something, you, the writer, want to present to an editor. Mentioning the occasion as quickly as possible grabs the reader's attention and hopefully, *holds it* until she finishes reading the inside. For a Birthday card, for example, the most obvious way, would be to simply start off "Happy Birthday!" and go right into the caption. Other opening phrases might include "Since it's your Birthday," "Now that you're a year older" or "Getting older isn't the horrible thing it's cracked up to be."

When you state the occasion up front, you define what the card is going to be. Starting with "Now that you're new parents" has the reader know this particular card is going to be about having a baby. You wouldn't write a caption, for example, that read:

O: Now that you're new parents, you'll have a lot more gray hair than before...
I: ...even though you only have one more candle on your cake than you did last year. Happy Birthday!

This caption doesn't hook the reader; it would only distract her. You started out promising one occasion; the entire outside caption signals this will be about new babies. The inside caption, however, doesn't make good on this promise.

Properly dividing and properly defining a caption are two technical areas in the business of writing greeting cards which you must practice and learn. Take heart! As in most other things, practice makes near-perfect and once you understand these concepts, they can take a back seat to the fun stuff of creating and selling your captions.

BAKER'S DOZEN EXERCISE: <u>LET'S DIVIDE!</u>

Read these complete captions and determine (by way of a slash mark) where the outside caption ends and the inside one begins.

1. Happy Birthday! You know, everything ages with time. I was looking in the mirror the other day and I noticed a wrinkle! I thought to myself, **My God,** my mirror's getting old! How about yours?

2. This Thanksgiving I vow to do better on my diet. I will not eat anything with the letter "x" in it.

3. Happy Mother's Day, Mom. Now that I'm older, I thought I'd test some of your theories and you know what? You were right. A person can't survive on potato chips alone.

4. Just a note from your daughter—Don't worry about sending more money so I can pay the rent. I met some nice boys in a fraternity who will let me move in for free.

5. It's Thanksgiving! Everything is in its place. One turkey in the oven, one turkey on the couch and a lot of turkeys on TV. Happy Thanksgiving!

6. Happy Birthday to the best-looking old person I know.

7.   Just think, your new baby may grow up to be a famous scientist or artist or even a renowned author and write a best seller telling the world how you screwed up its childhood.

8. Together you two can weather anything! Happy Anniversary!

9. Thanksgiving is when millions of Americans gorge themselves at dinner and then complain an hour later how slow the quarterback is.

10.   You know, birthdays coming once a year don't scare me

anymore. Wrinkles setting in and gray hair falling out don't scare me either. Miniskirts coming back, now **that** scares me! Oh well, Happy Birthday!

11. I understand you just paid for a new car, a new boat, and membership in a country club. Get Well Soon. Your doctor doesn't need anything else.

12. Glad to hear you're on the road to recovery!

13. Please write. Monroe could slice the catsup, but he just couldn't cut the mustard. I relish your letters.

ANSWERS:
<u>*LET'S DIVIDE!*</u>

1. Happy Birthday! You know, everything ages with time. I was looking in the mirror the other day and I noticed a wrinkle! I thought to myself, **My God,** / my mirror's getting old! How about yours? (© Oatmeal Studios)
*("Looking in the mirror and noticing" is the hook that causes the reader to think the wrinkles are on the person. **"My God"** reinforces the hook.)*

2. This Thanksgiving I vow to do better on my diet. / I will not eat anything with the letter "x" in it. (© Oatmeal Studios)
(Another division possibility could be after the word "anything.")

3. Happy Mother's Day, Mom. Now that I'm older, I thought I'd test some of your theories and you know what? / You were right. A person can't survive on potato chips alone. (© Oatmeal Studios)
(A second division possibility could be after the word "right.")

4. Just a note from your daughter——Don't worry about sending more money so I can pay the rent. / I met some nice boys in a fraternity who will let me move in for free.   (© Argus Communications)

5. It's Thanksgiving! Everything is in its place. / One turkey in the oven, one turkey on the couch and a lot of turkeys on TV. Happy Thanksgiving!
(© Oatmeal Studios)
(Even though the division here is evident, this caption needs a major tightening. The inside caption would flow much more smoothly if it read: I: A turkey in the oven, another on the couch and a bunch on TV.)

6. Happy Birthday **/** to the best-looking old person I know. (© Oatmeal Studios)

(Another possibility is after the words "best-looking.")

7. Just think, your new baby may grow up to be a famous scientist or artist or even a renowned author and write a best seller **/** telling the world how you screwed up its childhood. (© Sandra Louden)

(This caption generates the most discussion among my students. Many want to divide it after "author," but the words "write a best seller" flow quite naturally from the word "author," so the best division is after "seller.")

8. Together **/** you two can weather anything! Happy Anniversary! (© Current Inc.)

(This caption obviously depends on a visual; in this case, the picture showed two people in the rain under an umbrella. Another possibility would be to have the entire caption placed on the inside of the card.)

9. Thanksgiving is when millions of Americans gorge themselves at dinner and then complain an hour later **/** how slow the quarterback is. (© Sandra Louden)

(This is another caption that always brings some disagreement, as many students divide it after "dinner." However, the concept of "complaining an hour later" suggests complaining because of "gorging," which is, of course, the hook.)

10. You know, birthdays coming once a year don't scare me anymore. Wrinkles setting in and gray hair falling out don't scare me either. **/** Miniskirts coming back, now **that** scares me! Oh well, Happy Birthday! (© Argus)

11. I understand that you just paid for a new car, a new boat, and membership in a country club. **/** Get Well Soon. Your doctor doesn't need anything else.
(© Oatmeal Studios)

(I've included this caption on purpose to show you that for every rule, there's an exception. "Defining the occasion" in this case doesn't come until the reader opens the card. However, because of the unique nature of this caption, the card

itself helped clarify the occasion by showing two people entering a building clearly marked "Hospital." If you, the writer, wrote such a caption, you'd want to suggest some visual that would aid your words.)

12. Glad to hear you're on the road to recovery! (© Pawprints)
(The actual card carried this caption entirely on the inside with the outside visual showing an ambulance going down the road.)

13. Please write. Monroe could slice the catsup, but he just couldn't cut the mustard. / I relish your letters. (© Recycled Paper Greetings)
(This is a "cartoon card," where the entire cartoon block—visual and words—are on the outside of the card and the greeting card element comes in by the words carried on the inside, which complements the cartoon. Note the outside is a narrative; the inside is the personal, me-to-you message.)

THE THREE TYPES OF THINKING: BROADLY, VISUALLY, LITERALLY

THINKING BROADLY

Through the years, I've written many different types of captions and upon some analysis, discovered these captions can be broken into three basic types of thinking used to create them.   Often these ways of thinking overlap, which is one of the fun things about creativity—it's always out there bouncing around, waiting for the writer to catch it.

Let's turn to the first way you must think: *Broadly*. When you think broadly, you think horizontally, across the widest spectrum, finding references that most people can relate to and identify with. This goes back to what we discussed previously about rack impact. Since the product you're writing for has such a short time in which to grab someone's attention, your references (especially in the outside line) must be instantly recognizable, to-the-point and clear.

If, for example, you're writing a Father's Day card around the theme of "woodworking Dad," you'd want to use a "hammer and nail" reference rather than a "lathe and awl." Granted, it *feels* more creative to use the latter (you get to show off your woodworking knowledge), but it's much too obscure for the *second-and-a-half* attention-grabbing factor.   Save the lathe and awl for your short story, how-to article or novel.

The best way to initiate broad thinking is by the process known as brainstorming. You all know what brainstorming is and you've generally associated it with many people. As a solitary freelance writer, though, you'll need to develop brainstorming techniques while alone. However you jump-start those techniques is as unique to you as your own personality; but jump-start them you must to get that wide frame of reference so essential to a successful card caption.

Two operative words to remember about brainstorming: Get Involved. Let's say you have to come up with Thanksgiving captions. Watch every Thanksgiving television special there is. Volunteer at a hospital or school to help decorate for the holiday; you'll rub shoulders with others who'll have Thanksgiving on their minds and will be talking about their own holiday preparations.

Your library, as always is an invaluable source. Check out every November issue of any magazine you think might be relevant, especially general women's, food, travel and lifestyle magazines. Inundate yourself in Thanksgiving; involve all your senses to fully experience the holiday and write down every impression, every feeling you get from this involvement. This is a kind of brainstorming you can do yourself and the results will surprise you.

In an ideal situation, you would be able to call upon a group of brilliant, creative people, have them come to your home, allow them to toss valuable ideas around for an hour or two, and then chase them all out so you could write your captions in creative solitude. In the case of brainstorming, you'll have to compromise somewhat.

The advantage, however, is still on the side of the independent freelance writer.   We can involve ourselves as much—or as little—as we choose and we still have that precious, quiet time alone that every writer requires, not only for creative output, but for inward soul searching as well.

BAKER'S DOZEN EXERCISE:
<u>THINKING BROADLY</u>

Remembering that obscure, limited references have no place in a greeting card, you should use the following exercise to get you started Thinking Broadly.   Only go for the wide-reaching, universal answer.   This exercise can become a valuable reference sheet which you should use as a starting-off point as you begin writing your own captions. Suggestions for answers follow.

1. You're writing a Halloween card referring to mystery or "scary" writers. Name some.

2.   You've been asked to write a Father's Day card centering around "Boating Dad." Give some sailing terms, expressions or things associated with the sea.

3.   You need famous baseball players for a Brother Birthday card. Name some.

4. Valentine's Day makes us think of romance. Name three well-known couples.

5. Name five "doctors," fictional or real, for a Get Well card.

6.   You're asked to come up with a dieting card.   Give five luscious desserts everyone would recognize.

7. Name two famous dogs. Two horses. Two cats. Two pigs.

8. Your editor has a new line of cards revolving around computer themes. Give some "computerese" terms.

9.   Generation X (born between 1965 and 1981) is the next big card-buying group on the horizon. Give five Generation X terms or slang.

10.   Give three of the guiding principles of Kwanzaa and what

they mean.

11.   Your editor needs Graduation ideas.   List six things associated with graduations.

12. List seven things associated with secretaries and offices for Bosses' and Secretaries' Day.

13. You have to write a Thank You card. Say it in five different ways.

ANSWERS:
THINKING BROADLY

1. Stephen King, Edgar Allan Poe, Rod Serling, Agatha Christie, R.L. Stine.

2. Landlubber, "Old Salt," Bluebeard, Surf 'N Turf, "Sea Legs," Walking the Plank, Mizzen, Dry Dock, Schooner.

3. Babe Ruth, Lou Gehrig, Mickey Mantle, Jackie Robinson, Joe DiMaggio, Ty Cobb.

4. Romeo & Juliet, Napoleon & Josephine, Anthony & Cleopatra, Archie & Edith, Lucy & Ricky, Superman & Lois Lane, Dagwood & Blondie, Tarzan & Jane, Wilma & Fred (Flintstone), Bogie & Bacall, Popeye & Olive Oil.

5. Dr. Ruth, Marcus Welby, Dr. Seuss, Ben Casey, Dr. Spock, Dr. J., Dr. Jekyll, Dr. No, Dr. Strangelove, Doc Holliday, Spin Doctor, Dr. Pepper.

6. Chocolate Mousse, Baked Alaska, Cherries Jubilee, Devil's Food Cake, Lemon Meringue Pie.

7. Snoopy, Scooby-Doo, Toto, Lassie.   Mr. Ed, Flicka, Trigger. Garfield, Morris, Sylvester.   Miss Piggy, Porky, Wilbur, Arnold K. Ziffel (Green Acres).

8.   DOS, ROM, Motherboard, Low-Density Diskettes, Power Surge, Hard Drive, Crashed.

9. AUTHOR'S NOTE: This one always presents problems for my students. Is it time to brush up on your Generation X lingo? Remember, in a short time, this Generation will represent the majority of card buyers.   **Bit Spit** (Any form of digital correspondence), **Buds** (Friends), **Huppie** (Blend of hippie and yuppie, describing anyone upwardly mobile, but spending her spare time living like a hippie), **Ohnosecond** (Tiny fraction of time when you realize you've done something—especially on a

computer—that can't be undone), **Talk Outside One's Neck** (Xer's version of "Talking Out of Both Sides Of One's Mouth," meaning to lie or tease.).

10. UMOJA (Unity), NIA (Purpose), KUUMBA (Creativity).

11. Cap & Gown, Diploma, Tassel, Valedictorian, "Senior-itis," Pomp & Circumstance.

12. Dictaphone, Shorthand, Water Cooler, Office Parties, Football Pools, Switchboard Duty, FAX.

13. "Thanks A Million," "Thanks From The Bottom Of My Heart," Muchas Gracias," "Thanks A Bunch," "Much Obliged," "You Shouldn't Have," "Thanks A Heap."

THINKING VISUALLY

My ability to think visually has accounted for well over half my total greeting card sales. Whether you can actually draw is irrelevant—as long as you are able to **think in pictures**.

When you think visually, you focus on the card in its entirety. You see a picture in your mind and then come up with the words to accompany or "flesh out" that picture. Sometimes the reverse happens. You hear a phrase or sentence you know would make a terrific caption, but without a visual to help it along, the words are obscure.

Take a caption such as: "It's OK. You can light your candles anytime! Happy Birthday!" Nice; but what's the connecting, cohesive factor to have it make sense?   The picture, of course. Add the description of the visual—a fireman, holding a hose, aimed directly at the reader—and you've got yourself a greeting card.

Visual thinking (and its counterpart, literal thinking, which we cover next) are what cartoonists use in their line of work as well. Their visuals enhance the humor and often the visual **is** the humor, without any words used at all.   Characters like Ziggy, Garfield and Charlie Brown are as much visual characters as they are talking ones.

Visual captions are especially important in **alternate products** such as mugs, memo pads, calendars or blank note cards.   These products often rely on a picture and a brief phrase or expression to get the sentiment across.   If you don't draw or sketch, you'll merely describe what visual you have in mind, right before the caption.   Since most greeting card copy is sent on index cards (more on the actual submission process later), you'll have to develop the knack of succinct and to-the-point description.

With the expanded popularity of photographed cards and the peculiar genre of card best exemplified by cartoonist Gary Larson's *The Far Side*, visual thinking must be an integral part of every successful greeting card writer's "thinking repertoire."

BAKER'S DOZEN PLUS TWO EXERCISE: <u>THINKING VISUALLY</u>

I've designed the following exercise to help you begin the process of thinking visually. Below are captions which need a visual description to make their meaning clear. Your job is to describe an appropriate scene which would fit the words and do so in no more than two sentences. Suggestions for answers follow.

1. "Who are the turkeys, which ones are the clowns and where are the jerks?"

2. "Make that one dozen roses. The card reads: To My Wife!"

3. "I love reflecting on you at Christmas!"

4. "Hope the fun is piled high today. Happy Birthday!"

5. "I love you t-h-i-i-i-s much!"

6. "Now THIS is what I call Holiday Shopping!"

7. "Congratulations on another year well done!"

8. "We're making no bones about it...Have A Happy Birthday!"

9. "Dieting or Non-Dieting"

10. "Unaccustomed as I am to public **sweeping**, I'd still like to wish you a Happy Birthday!"

11. "Ours...is such a cultivated friendship"

12. "After all, I did win the race! Happy Easter!"

13. "I should have asked for a job description"

14. "If only I could turn up the brightness as easily."

15. "How can I keep tabbies on you if you never write?!"

ANSWERS:
THINKING VISUALLY

1. Woman brings her child to the office. Co-workers are all at their desks as the child says loudly: "Who are the turkeys, etc." (Calendar caption) .

2. Woman is sitting at her desk with telephone nestled to her ear and whispering into the receiver. February 14th is on her calendar in the background.

3. Glass ornament is hanging on the tree while two people, obviously in love, are looking at their combined reflection.

4. Ice cream cone piled with many different colored scoops of ice cream. (Juvenile Birthday)

5. Picture of octopus stretching out all eight legs for a super hug.

6. Woman is soaking in a hot bubble bath with December catalogues lying all around her.

7. Photograph shows sizzling, grilled steak on the barbecue.

8. Dogs with bones in their mouths looking at the reader. (Birthday) OR Skeletons holding hands grinning and standing in a row. (Birthday; or omit the Birthday tag line & substitute Happy Halloween)

9. Waitress is giving woman a raised-eyebrow look as she's waiting to be seated in a restaurant. Prominent "Smoking" & "Non-Smoking Section" signs adorn the room.

10. Janitor is leaning on a broom, looking at the reader.

11. Photograph or drawing of many different flowers blooming in a garden.

12.   Turtle is holding a sign which reads "Easter Tortoise" with the words: "It's **finally** my turn to wish you a Happy Easter." Exhausted hare is coming in second at the finish line.

13. Woman is in her kitchen doing many things at once—washing the dog, talking on the phone, cooking dinner, tying children's shoelaces, etc.

14. Woman is looking at her husband sleeping on the couch as the television blares in the background.

15.   Cat perched on top of mailbox, looking sad.

THINKING LITERALLY

Thinking literally is my favorite way of thinking. When I lecture, I tell students the simplest way to begin training your brain to think literally, is to think of English as your second tongue, rather than your first.

Pretend you're a foreign exchange student and someone tells you a story and ends with: "He really got in hot water over that!" Well. You know what "hot water" is and you understand the concept of "getting in," so you put two and two together (another phrase that could easily be taken literally) and are certain you've just come up with a "he literally got in a tub of hot water and became soaking wet" four—but, of course, that's not what happened at all, is it?

Whether the pretend exchange student in you realized it or not, you've just thought literally—which is the type of thinking that produces so many of those very funny, *groaner* captions (they make you groan out loud). Think about some of these phrases in a literal mode: Giving someone the cold shoulder. Turning over a new leaf. A shot in the arm. Quite different from the way you normally—or figuratively—think of these common expressions.

When you, the writer, take every word or phrase and apply the most literal meaning you can to it, you produce that *hook* or fooler we spoke of earlier. This, in turn, causes the unsuspecting reader to misassociate the caption's meaning—which is where the humor comes in. Your outside caption sets forth a very straightforward statement and the reader jumps to the conventional conclusion of what he expects the inside caption to be. The humor, of course, is that the inside caption is quite unconventional (due entirely to this concept of literal thinking).

Let's look at a specific example, seeing only the outside line at first:

O: *Now that you're new parents, you'll have to budget a lot more of your time and money. Just remember the old saying, "Charity begins at home...*

What is the key phrase in this caption around which a writer could build the humor? You should have said, "Charity begins at home." Now what is the specific or pivotal word in the phrase? It should be fairly obvious the word is "charity." This is the word around which you build your literal meaning.

And the inside line then reads:

I: *...and goes off to college 18 years later. Congratulations!*

Why is this caption funny? We normally think of "charity" as money given for a good cause or as a form of selfless volunteerism. The writer has used "charity," however, as a synonym for one's own child living off Mom and Dad for 18 years before going to college. The writer has hooked or fooled the reader; a reader who has been conditioned to accept "charity" for its usual, conventional meaning.

Let's look at several other outside captions to see where literal thinking occurs. First, find the phrase that should be taken literally and then see if that literal meaning jump-starts a possible hook that leads you into a logical inside-line conclusion.

O: *When you go out with a guy, remember to judge him by the company he keeps...*

O: *Another birthday and you look like a million!*

O: *Despite being another year older, you're holding up well...*

O: *I have good news and bad news. The good news is I dropped some weight...*

In the first example, we find a well-known saying "judge him by the company he keeps." The word *company*, in this case, means people. But what other meaning does the word company have besides this one? Can it also mean a business organization or industrial firm?

"Looking like a million" used to carry the figurative, additional word, "bucks" meaning, "you look terrific." Now, however, because the word "bucks" has been dropped (but the meaning is still intact), it's open to another humorous interpretation.

"Holding up well" figuratively means you're doing okay, you're feeling well. Think of a body part that might need "holding up" and you may arrive quite naturally at the inside caption.

And finally, when we use the word "drop" in connection with weight, we mean "loss." But what happens when we "drop" a vase? Do we "lose" it or does gravity pull it down to the ground where it then shatters? If an astute writer thinks in terms of gravity, rather than loss, the inside caption becomes obvious. And here are the inside lines:

I: *...and the company he owns, the companies he's merged...*

I: *...give or take a year. (Another literal possibility: ...after taxes)*

I: *...new bra?*

I: *...the bad news is it dropped from my waist to my thighs.*

A second form of literal thinking occurs when the writer combines the literal and visual forms of thought. In the above examples, the words stood by themselves. They were immediately apparent and didn't require the writer to describe or sketch a visual to make them clear to an editor.

Remember the caption I told you about in the introduction? *These days it's getting tougher and tougher to make ends meet* is the perfect example of not only visual thinking, but the combination of the visual and literal. Thinking visually, we describe a woman trying to touch her toes, but not succeeding. Using our literal thinking skills, we hook the reader by taking a phrase generally associated with financial blues and turning it into one having to do with exercise.

Think Broadly:
Brainstorm
Think Visually:
Get A Picture
Think Literally:
Pull Apart Every Expression

AN EVEN DOZEN EXERCISE: THINKING LITERALLY

To help you switch your thinking from the conventional to the literal, below is an exercise listing common expressions. Your natural inclination will be to think of them first in their figurative sense; however, as a caption writer, you must train yourself to see their literal meaning as well.

Describe them in their most literal sense and then try to find an appropriate connection with an occasion for a greeting card. My suggestions for this exercise follow.

1. Bent Out Of Shape

2. Face Value

3. Fringe Benefits

4. Speaking Out Of Both Sides Of One's Mouth

5. Cutting Corners

6. In The Same Boat

7. Hit The Nail On The Head

8. Close Call

9. Nothing To Sneeze At

10. Let The Cat Out Of The Bag

11. Get A Grip!

12. It's A Dog Eat Dog World!

ANSWERS:
THINKING LITERALLY

1. One of my best-selling captions featured the bon mot: *Happy are the flexible, for we shall never be bent out of shape.* The phrase is a natural one for an alternate card with the theme of exercising.

2. "Face value" could certainly be used with a statement about wrinkles, crow's feet, etc., which in turn could be turned into a birthday caption on the joys of aging.

3. "Fringe benefits" could suggest scanty, fringed clothing, which would be perfect for a suggestive anniversary card.

4. This expression generally implies fibbing or lying, so a possible use for "speaking out of both sides of one's mouth" could be a new twist on lying about one's age.

5. Any phrase with money or cash cited in it, such as "cutting corners," can be brainstormed to perk up the old standby greeting card theme of "Sorry, no money in this card!" It can also fit the varied occasions of graduation, new job or even new parenting. ("Look how much baby is going to cost you through the years" theme.)

6. "In the same boat" implies a shared experience, generally a negative one. A logical choice here might be a caption on coping and "getting through it together" friendship card.

7. "Hitting the nail on the head" conjures up such a clear image and would be great for a Father's Day or Father birthday card carrying the "fix-it Dad" theme.

8. "Close call" reminds me of an auctioneer on the podium surrounded by expensive antiques. Antiques call to mind age and of course, age reminds me of the most popular occasion of all—birthdays.

9. "Sneezing?" Catching a cold? Sick? Obviously, a get well caption could be your brainstorming start-off point here.

10. When you "let the cat out of the bag," you let a secret slip. Do some people try to keep their age a secret?

11. "Get a grip" could be brainstormed around a sports theme, such as a grip on a tennis racket or golf clubs. It could be used for a number of occasions, including birthday, new job, lighthearted friendship, etc.

12. This expression seems to suggest a congratulations card telling the recipient he's come out on top in this "dog eat dog world" we live in.

TRICKS OF THE TRADE: PUNS, EXPRESSIONS, INITIALS

PUNS
The Good, The Bad, The Fatal (Including "The Ten Most 'Unwanted' List!")

In any creative field, from carpentry to cooking, there are certain tricks of the trade which professional people fall back on without hesitation from time to time. If performed correctly, these tricks almost always ensure success; whether making a soufflé or building a desk, as they help you get started without wasting extra time or energy.

It's no different with greeting card writing. Occasionally you may find you've stumbled into a temporary creative slump (this is **not** writer's block, by the way!) and if you do, these tricks will help pull you out by giving a definite format and boundaries to your writing efforts. These tricks also help by taking the pressure off; pressure which usually comes when you are writing absolutely **nothing**, simply because you've convinced yourself you can't think of anything to write. (The quintessential Catch-22 situation) Once you understand these tricks, you'll be able to slip into them as if they were a pair of comfortable old slippers.

First, you should have a working knowledge of the

pun. Puns, **when used effectively**, are an extremely important part of card writing. The operative words here: used effectively.

You should avoid two major pitfalls when writing a caption that includes a pun. The first is triteness. Let's face it, there are puns that have been around since the birth of greeting cards and as a professional, you should *never, ever, under any circumstances* (Did I emphasize that enough?) submit these to an editor. You may actually see some of these puns in today's greeting cards (often in boxed sets), but these are part of huge caption databases that companies pull from when they re-issue cards. No editor will shell out cash to a freelancer who tries to pass these off as her own original work.

What are some of these puns you should avoid? My Ten Most Unwanted List is as follows:

>   1. "Ewe" for "you" as in "Wishing EWE were here." This sentiment is always accompanied by cute, fuzzy sheep.

>   2. "Hare" for "hair." This sentiment is always accompanied by cute, furry bunnies.

>   3. "Bear-y" or "Berry" for "Very." I am really BERRY sick of this pun.

>   4. "Bunny" for "Body" as in "You're SOMEBUNNY special!" Another one for the Brain Dead Hall of Fame.

>   5. "Egg" for the prefix "-ex" as in "You're so EGGCEPTIONAL!" or "You're so EGGCITING!" Unfortunately, this pun is neither.

6. "Socks" or "Sox" for "Sex" as in "SOX Appeal." Where's the barf bag?

7. "Sax" for "Sex" as in "SAX Appeal." This pun has **no** appeal, sax or otherwise.

8. "Tanks" for "Thanks" as in "Many TANKS!" Tanks, but No Tanks!"

9. "Feline" for "Feeling" used in "Hope you're FELINE fine!" I'm feline rather sick after that, tank you!

10. "Witches" for "Wishes." This one, of course, is always reserved for Halloween. It should be— it fits right in with all the other horrible stuff.

The other pitfall in writing puns is just the opposite. These are the puns that are too far-fetched; these "reach too far." Here the writer is trying to be too clever and comes up with an elaborate network of like-sounding syllables that no one "gets."

Unfortunately, it's harder to pinpoint an obscure pun than a trite one that's seen everywhere. I've given you a few below and if, at any time, you're scratching your head, wondering "Huh?", you proven my point.

She's made a lot of dumb remarks in her lifetime, so please don't **quota.**

Any country that installs prophylactic machines in its restrooms is asking for **condomnation** status.

It's possible to tame a Peruvian camel, but you must be careful not to **a llama.**

> The bosses' daughter doesn't need to worry about wearing asbestos...she's **fireproof**.

Besides being far-fetched and not funny, you may have noticed one other important point. These puns really don't have a purpose other than to make the reader groan. As a greeting card writer whose uppermost concern is with the me-to-you, sendability factor, you have to be careful not to let the reader with a feeling of "so what?" .

✍ *You Must Have A <u>REASON</u> To Send A Greeting Card!* ✍

So, where is a happy medium between trite, overused puns and the obscure, silly ones? One definitely exists and the writer who finds that middle ground will find himself selling his puns almost faster than he can write them.

Here are a few examples of successful puns.

> O: You'll find the hardest thing about graduation is leaving home...
> I: ...and giving up all those fridge benefits. Congratulations!

> O: Visual shows woman trying on a pair of pants that are too small.
>   Caption: I don't know about you...
> I: ...but lately I find I'm in a much higher slacks bracket than ever before.

O: Visual shows woman looking at her sleeping children.
            No caption.
I: No noise is good noise, don't you agree?

One final note: "Puns" and "play on words" are often used interchangeably, but there is a subtle difference. A "play on words" is what we looked at in Literal Thinking; the writer is simply "playing around with words," not changing them. In a pun, she is actually coming up with a new word to replace the one generally associated with the phrase or expression.

EXPRESSIONS

The clever writer should not only look at expressions with an eye toward how they can be applied literally, she should also be able to pick out the key words of an expression and see how substituting a different word could change the meaning.

Let's look at a common saying:

Behind every successful man is a woman

What are the key words in this phrase? They're fairly easy to pick out, aren't they? "Successful," "man," and "woman." How could this expression be changed by substituting some or all of the key words?

Behind every successful cat is an obedient owner
Behind every successful woman is her Mom
Behind every successful woman is herself
Behind every ozone hole is a successful spray can

Substitution itself isn't the only tool a writer can use in working with common expressions. Take the following:

A taste of your own medicine.

By merely adding several words, you have a clever caption tied into a card for Nurses' Day.

Nurses give people a taste of their own medicine.

You can see there are endless possibilities in taking common expressions, phrases, even slogans and substituting, adding or deleting words from them. But do you have a clue just how many expressions there are to choose from out there?

On the next page is a list you'll find helpful to get you thinking along the "expression line." My students are often surprised by this list; one I tell them is nothing more than a mere starting point in a language that is filled with such rich, vibrant sayings. You'll want to refer to this list frequently in personal brainstorming sessions.

50 EXPRESSIONS

1) Friends don't let friends drive drunk!
2) A mind is a terrible thing to waste.
3) Never send a boy to do a man's job.
4) It's 11:00. Do you know where your children are?
5) You can't have your cake & eat it too.
6) Just say no!
7) Functionally illiterate.
8) Nice guys finish last.
9) Winning isn't everything. It's the only thing.
10) Beauty is in the eye of the beholder.
11) This is where we separate the men from the boys.
12) Above & beyond the call of duty.
13) A search for identity.
14) What's a nice girl like me doing in a place like this?
15) Boy meets girl/boy loses girl/boy gets girl.
16) The spur of the moment.
17) A fate worse than death.
18) Don't drink & drive.
19) Been there. Done that.
20) Living beyond one's means.
21) No more Mr. Nice Guy.
22) Life is just a bed of roses.
23) Life in the fast lane.
24) Clean up your act!
25) What goes around, comes around!
26) I never met a man I didn't like!
27) Live happily ever after.
28) Love, honor and cherish (obey).
29) Driving while under the influence...
30) The spirit is willing, but the flesh is weak.
31) Never judge a book by its cover.
32) The hand that rocks the cradle rules the world.
33) Get your act together!
34) Have gun, will travel
35) Real men don't eat quiche.
36) A man's home is his castle.
37) A woman's place is in the home.
38) Children should be seen & not heard.

39) Nothing ventured, nothing gained.
40) To err is human, to forgive divine.
41) Mixing business with pleasure.
42) Man cannot live by bread alone.
43) Pulling a few strings.
44) The way to a man's heart is through his stomach.
45) Still crazy after all these years.
46) Making the world safe for democracy.
47) It's a dirty job, but somebody's got to do it.
48) I'll hate myself in the morning.
49) All dressed up and no place to go.
50) In for a penny, in for a pound.

INITIALS

Closely related to the substitution of key words in common phrases and expressions is the complete changing of words from readily-recognizable initials. In our language, we use abbreviations in the form of initials all the time—from the ubiquitous OK (which came from a 19th century presidential campaign where the words *Oll Korrect* were deliberately misspelled) to the equally common TV for television.

Again, the hook (either humorous or caring) comes in because the unexpected occurs; the reader expects the initials to stand for one set of words, while the writer has changed these words to fit a sendable occasion.

Take the initials, TLC, which, of course, stand for "Tender Loving Care" and are usually coupled with the introductory words, "plenty of..." For the same nursing assignment in which I sold "taste of their own medicine," I also came up with:

Nurses give their patients plenty of TLC:
Thermometers, Locals and Catheters

For a teaching note pad or mug, you could write:
Teachers give their students plenty of TLC:
Tests, Lectures and Criticism

A possible sporting theme might be:
Tennis players give their opponents plenty of TLC:
Topspin, Lobs and Cannonballs

For a Friendship card, there is:
> O: *Even though we're modern women, we still deserve plenty of TLC...*
> I: *...Totally Luscious Chocolate!*

As you can see, the creative possibilities are endless, although as in the other writing tricks we've discussed, there is the same word of caution. The words must be appropriate to the theme and cannot seem forced or contrived. They must flow naturally and logically to create a humorous or caring alternate meaning. Also, the initials themselves must be instantly recognizable by the majority of people. You might come up with a brilliant caption based on IAS, but how many people know (or care) that IAS originally stood for Indicated Air Speed?

Just as in the previous section, I've given you a list of common initials, followed by their generally accepted meaning. Work on finding new, exciting words to substitute for the conventional ones. Once again, this list is merely a jumping off point and you should add to it as you hear and see other examples.

40 INITIALS

1) I.O.U.

2) R.S.V.P.

3) V.I.P.

4) R.I.P.

5) S.R.O.

6) T & A

7) P.M.S.

8) D.O.A.

9) S.O.B.

10) B.M.O.C.

11) F.B.I.

12) C.P.A.

13) I.R.S.

14) P.O.'d

15) E.R.A.

16) P.S.

17) The Three R's

18) S.A.S.E.

19) B.S.

20) F.Y.I.

21) C.Y.A.

22) A.B.C.'s

23) P.D.Q.

24) A.S.A.P.

25) T.N.T.

26) D.W.I.

27) K.O.'d

28) P.T.A.

29) U.F.O.

30) T.G.I.F.

31) S.W.A.K.

32) S.N.A.F.U.

33) C.P.R.

34) S&L Crisis

35) S & M

36) VCR

37) MVP

38) B.Y.O.B.

39) ESP

40) R & R

WHAT THESE INITIALS MEAN

1. I Owe You
2. Respondez s'il vous plait (Please reply)
3. Very Important Person
4. Rest In Peace
5. Standing Room Only
6. *Do I really have to explain this one?*
7. Pre-Menstrual Syndrome
8. Dead On Arrival
9. *See #6.*
10. Big Man On Campus
11. Federal Bureau Of Investigation
12. Certified Public Accountant
13. Internal Revenue Service
14. P***** Off
15. Equal Rights Amendment/Earned Run Average
16. Post Script
17. Readin', Ritin', Rithmetic
18. Self-Addressed, Stamped Envelope
19. *Another one you know if you've lived on this planet*
20. For Your Information
21. Cover Your A**
22. The Fundamentals of Anything
23. Pretty Darned Quick
24. As Soon As Possible
25. Trinitrotoluene (Yes I had to look it up!)
26. Driving While Intoxicated/Driving While under the Influence
27. Knocked Out
28. Parent Teacher Association
29. Unidentified Flying Object
30. Thank God It's Friday
31. Sealed With A Kiss
32. Situation Normal, All Fouled (Polite Word) Up
33. Cardiac Pulmonary Resuscitation
34. Savings & Loan Crisis
35. SadoMasochism
36. Video Cassette Recorder
37. Most Valuable Player
38. Bring Your Own Bottle
39. Extra-Sensory Perception
40. Rest & Relaxation

TRADITIONAL VERSE: A BRIEF NOD TO THE PAST

Traditional verse has been called the "heart of the industry" and once upon a time, that statement was certainly true. Browse through any card shop and you'll notice the traditional rhymed and metered poetry format is definitely present on the racks.

Let's take a random look, however, at various writer's guidelines I've received from different companies through the years:

A greeting card is a form of communication. It should sound like a person talking.

Remember that we're not interested in long, rhymed verse or prose. Most of our cards feature one or two concise lines.

Submit verses from one to four lines in length that are simple and to-the-point ideas...Rhymed verse is not generally used.

Shorter verses are better than long, wordy verses. We do not need poetry.

We only need studio humor.

> *We will consider poetry, since it's appropriate for a certain consumer group, but it isn't what we generally find suitable for...our card lines.*

You should be aware, because of comments like these—and also from the various guidelines and needs lists you've received—that, in general, editors do not look for traditional verse from their freelance writers. As I stressed, however, in the introduction, companies and what they need, can and do change. If you write poetry, by all means, don't stop.

As in contemporary prose and humor, there are certain rules in writing greeting card poetry. First, avoid poetic flights of fancy. You're not writing for Byron, Shelley or Keats; you're writing for the general public. **Yours is still a personal message, conveying a wish, compliment or greeting, which just happens to be written in metered rhyme.** If your poetic language sounds stilted, your message will sound ridiculous instead of sincere. Think back. When was the last time you said to your neighbor: *Methinks you should cut your grass!* ; asked your children: *Are you traveling o'er your friend's house today?* ; or commented on a criminal whose photo was flashed on the news: *Well, he certainly looks like a ne'er-do-well!* ?

You're laughing, but **the** most common reason that greeting card poetry is rejected is **antiquated word usage** (followed closely by forced rhyme and meter). Beginning writers are often so concerned with words rhyming and meters being mathematically correct, they allow these factors to override what should be uppermost in their mind; namely, the message, which must be simple, yet sincere; poetic, yet natural.

In poetry, more than any other type of writing, it's vital you read your work out loud. Better yet, have someone read your poetry cold, out loud, back to you. If a friend can read through it easily, without stumbling or hesitating over the rhyme or the rhythm, your verse is one step closer to being a hit with an editor.

One last thought on traditional verse before we move to contemporary prose: most books on writing poetry advise you to get a rhyming dictionary. I find such advice to be a double-edged sword. If you use the rhyming dictionary as an aid, then fine. However, if you find yourself scanning the book to give you ideas for a theme, then forget it. You'll end up writing a poem for Father's Day saying you're so **glad** you have a **Dad** who's better than any in **Trinidad**. Mom will suffer a similar fate as you tell her you've never had a **qualm** telling her she's the best **Mom**, alive or **embalmed**. (OK, so it's an extreme example, but you catch the drift here)

Remember, even in the language of poetry with its rhymes, rhythms and sometimes inverted word orders, your message must still come across as genuine, sincere, heartfelt.

✒ WOULD I PURCHASE THE VERSE I'VE JUST WRITTEN? ✒

CONTEMPORARY PROSE: SOFT, SWEET, SALABLE

If you try writing traditional verse and you just can't seem to come up with the natural feeling you desire, don't despair. There is a happy medium between the rhymed, metered verse we've just discussed and the humor so prevalent on today's racks, known as contemporary prose. (Sometimes also referred to as soft social expression or conversational prose)

Best defined as non-rhyming, short, direct snippets of caring, contemporary prose gives a kind of mini slice-of-life vignette bringing a wish, a word of encouragement, a sharing of love. There is humor to be found in contemporary prose, but it's the soft, sweet, cuddly humor often associated with animals or children. It's the kind of humor you send to your Great-Aunt Myrna.

Contemporary prose may be used for any occasion. Its versatility and wide range of style also make it the perfect "break" from studio humor when the writer is temporarily "funnied out."

Let's look at a few examples of contemporary prose.

O: We're so close, that even when we're far apart...
I: ...you don't seem far away.

O: Your friendship...
I: ...fits so comfortably into my life.

> O: *Of all the things I've ever said to you, only one*
> *really matters...*
> I: *...I love you.*

These particular captions all revolve around the theme of friendship. What else do you notice? All are quite personal, conveying an extremely warm, complimentary glow from sender to receiver. Each sentiment is only one sentence and none is the least bit complicated. They all sound as if a person is talking; there is nothing stilted or contrived in the language used to convey the message.

Seasonals are another area where contemporary prose works well.

> O: *He knows if you've been bad or good...*
> I: *Hope your Christmas is merry, anyway!*

> O: *No caption. Appropriate graphics.*
> I: *Your gift of love has given me a lifetime of smiles!*
> *Have a beautiful Mother's Day.*

> O: *Thanksgiving is a time for Family, Friends and*
> *Food...*
> I: *...in that order.*

> O: *Hanukkah...a tradition of freedom, courage and*
> *peace.*
> I: *A time of renewed faith and hope. Have a Joyous*
> *Celebration.*

After reading these examples, what words would you use to describe contemporary prose?

Straightforward, honest, simple might be three. Also, the conversational tone is what makes these sentiments personal and appealing.

The most successful approach to this writing style is to image a specific person you know and to write that card directly to that person. Remember, any emotion you have, has been experienced by thousands of others. As a writer, you have the responsibility to express that emotion so that others can adopt it as their own.

Through your words, relationships will be resumed, bridges built, fences torn down, apologies given and accepted. You are the silent third person, the anonymous voice helping two people communicate and connect. Sincerity and simplicity—often with a pinch of humor added—are your biggest allies. With the exception of sympathy or serious illness cards, humor—however gentle or sweet—can and should find its way into as much of your writing as possible. As a writer, you should always be mindful of humor's immense power not only to entertain, but to heal.

I use the following questions in my classes to elicit some personal brainstorming for this softer side of greeting cards. Your answers will be as unique as your own personality.

1. What is a friend.
2. Why has our particular friendship endured when others have not?
3. What is a baby?
4. What does being a parent mean?
5. What is a father's love?

6. Why is a father's love different from a mother's? Or is it?
7. What are five synonyms for the word *appreciation*?
8. What is growing older?
9. What does turning 40 mean? Why is it more poignant than turning 30?
10. Why do some "good-byes" hurt?
11. What are the things people are thankful for at Thanksgiving and why?
12. What is Hanukkah?
13. What does Easter mean?
14. A couple celebrates their Silver Wedding Anniversary. Why is that special?
15. What does it mean to be Irish? If you're not Irish, what do you think accounts for the wonderful, constant pride in their heritage?

Answering these questions and others like them should start you on a personal, soul-searching journey that may lead to some exciting creativity, excellent captions and ultimately, a nice paycheck.

PART FOUR
Go (We Sell!)

NUTS & BOLTS:
SUBMITTING TO AN EDITOR

If you've followed this book as I've intended, by now you've sent out for guidelines, you've scoured card racks and spinners and practiced the various exercises, simultaneously jotting down your own ideas in anticipation of sending out your first batch of material.

Well, guess what? You're now at one of the most exciting points in your career. You're ready to submit ideas to an editor.

And as any good salesman knows, the presentation of material is a vital part of eventual sales success. Naturally, the ideas themselves are the most important; no matter how you try and dress it up, a bad idea just won't sell. However, many good ideas have been doomed from the start as well, because the writer didn't take a few extra minutes for a professional showing.

There is a specific format most companies require for reviewing a freelancer's work. Even with the advent of faxed and e-mail submissions, the majority of your ideas will probably be sent on those 3x5" index cards we talked about earlier. (These should, by the way, be **cards**, as opposed to slips of paper, which are too flimsy and transparent for a professional look.)

Here are some other points to keep in mind when submitting your work:

↗ Even though many companies ask for "between 10 and 20 ideas" sent in a single envelope, eleven (11) ideas plus your SASE will get you the most for your first class stamp. Sending out this unconventional number gives you a "free" batch every tenth submission. Often, it's the 11th idea that sells.

↗ Neatness still counts! Put yourself in front of 25% of all ideas submitted and just be neat. It sounds so basic, yet **one quarter** of all submissions come to an editor scrawled in pencil on the backs of envelopes or on loose scraps of paper, misspelled, smudged, soiled by coffee cup rings. Many arrive minus a name or address or with an undersized return envelope. Put yourself in an editor's place. Would you be inclined to buy ideas from a writer who gave this sort of presentation?

↗ We define "neatness" as typewritten or computer-generated copy, or copy hand-printed in block letters, **in ink**. Block letters don't mean square "S's" or "C's." They are even, conventionally-shaped letters easily read by everyone.

These are block letters!

↗ Your index cards should be unlined, white or creme-colored. Companies do not want hot pink or lime green index cards. In other words, don't use gimmicks to sell your ideas. Allow the creativity to shine in your **writing!**

↗ Information contained on the card should be typed horizontally, not vertically. An example of a submitted idea will look like this:

PCC-023 (Birthday - Sister)

O: Happy Birthday to a Sister who's not only bright and beautiful, but organized and efficient too!

I: You did remember to buy a present for yourself, didn't you?!?

> Your Name
> Address
> Area Code/Phone #
> Social Security # (Optional)

- The code number used in the above example is a code of your own making. I generally pick two or three letters from a card company's name that immediately suggests its identity. In this case, PCC could be Pittsburgh Card Company (no such animal) and "023" means it would be the 23rd idea sent to that company.
- Once you begin a regular working relationship with a company, no note of explanation is needed when sending your ideas. It's not rude to simply put your ideas (along with your SASE) in an envelope and send them.
- And while it goes without saying (I'll say it anyway), always have a duplicate copy of anything you've sent. ALWAYS!

REMEMBER:
ONE IDEA PER INDEX CARD, NO MATTER HOW SHORT THE IDEA!

MISTAKES BEGINNERS MAKE

This part of my greeting card course—common beginning mistakes (and its flip side, *Why Ideas Don't Sell*)—is a favorite among my students. After years of talking with editors, I've compiled a list of their most frequent complaints regarding the submission foibles of their writers. You'll make your share of mistakes in the beginning; everyone does. Hopefully, however, they won't be *these* mistakes.

- The writer sends a "batch" of 200 ideas all at once, thinking the editor must buy something from all that material. In reality, the sheer number of cards spilling out in a heap on an editor's desk, will turn her off immediately. If she actually does start to read this "batch" (and many won't), you can be sure if the first two or three ideas are no good, she'll never get to Idea #139.

- On the opposite end of the spectrum, the writer has **one** terrific idea. She is extremely protective of this single idea and she's sure it has never been done or even thought of. Why? She's never, ever seen it on the rack. Generally, in this case, the writer goes so far as to call the editor, wishing to describe the one idea over the phone. **Nothing brands you as an amateur more quickly than the "one-idea caller."** Editors, especially in big card companies, get at least two or three of these calls a week. No legitimate editor will even listen to a verbal idea and any writer who phones with this in mind is sure to get a curt cut-off.

- The writer sends her ideas with insufficient postage, neglects to include an SASE—or includes a return envelope with no postage—and stuffs her ideas in an absurdly small envelope. Misspelled words and lumpy correction fluid dot the surface of the index card. The editor also knows what kind of jelly the writer had for breakfast. This scenario falls under the heading of neatness and attention to detail. Remember, most editors are former English majors and phrases like *"Dad and myself"* (instead of "Dad and I") or *"Your tops in my book!"* (instead of the contraction "You're") will only decrease your chances for a sale. It takes such a tiny extra effort to be professional—which simply means, BE NEAT and BE ACCURATE!

✔ Included with her submissions, the writer attaches a note saying: *"I've made copies of all my ideas, so I'll know if you publish one without paying for it."* This is my favorite mistake of all because it's so incredibly dumb. After implying the editor is a thief ready to rip her off, does this writer really expect to sell anything?

✔ The writer includes a full-size letter stating: "Enclosed is a batch of ideas" and signs her name. Period. An editor handles literally thousands of slips of paper daily. She wants to be able to slit open an envelope, look through the ideas and evaluate them with the least possible hassle. Unfolding a letter that tells her the obvious only wastes her time. If you have a specific comment or question pertinent to your work, a brief note is fine. Otherwise, just send the ideas with an SASE. It will be appreciated more than you'll ever know!

✔ The writer lists the royalties she wants to receive and spells out what rights she's willing to sell. The hard fact here is, most card companies buy all rights and pay no royalties, only a flat, one-time fee. Yours is a work-for-hire relationship and as a beginner, that policy is not negotiable. Keep it in perspective—you're basically writing a sentence or two, nothing more. Your caption isn't going to be the next cable TV Movie Of The Week. Work hard, set your sights high; but please, know the fine line between having confidence in your work and being obnoxious about it.

WHY IDEAS DON'T SELL

Greeting card sentiments are rejected for a variety of reasons. Below are listed some of the more common ones. Again, talking with a variety of editors, reading hundreds of guidelines through the years and remembering my own mistakes have helped in the compilation of this list. Avoid these errors and you'll save yourself time and postage, as well as making your way that much faster to the all-important, first sale.

- Ideas need to have a purpose. They need to be "sendable" with that strong me-to-you flavor. Writing a joke, no matter how funny, is not a personal communication between sender and recipient.

- Are your ideas funny? Or are they merely silly and nonsensical? Would you buy a card containing the caption you've just written? Would you like to receive the card you've just written?

- Are your ideas appropriate for the company? This can't be stressed enough. No matter how cute or original your pun is, if the company doesn't publish puns, you will not sell it! By the same token, don't send risqué ideas to a company that publishes family or religious-oriented material and vice versa. Be professional! Know what the editor wants, follow the guidelines and send your ideas accordingly.

- The idea is good, but too limited. An example of this would be a small company that publishes baby cards, but whose resources don't permit a separate card specifically for boy or girl babies. If you send an idea stressing cute baby girls dressed in pink, as much as the editor might like it, she won't buy it.

↗ The idea was good once upon a time, but is now so old it creaks. The #1 comment an editor will write on a rejected idea: "It's been done."

↗ The idea is too risqué, gross or mean. Editors are leery of publishing mean-spirited, extremely insulting captions and their place in the market is more limited than you might think. A shared laugh, poking gentle fun at both sender and receiver, is much preferred.

↗ The idea is too long and complicated for the format of a card. If the verse is good, but requires 75 words to get the concept across, it won't fly as a greeting card. Always keep in mind the potential rack impact of every caption you write.

↗ And finally, your idea is really terrific, short, appropriate, original and catchy, but still gets rejected. In that case, it's probably got nothing to do with the idea itself, but with external factors, such as how many ideas an editor is allowed to purchase within any given time frame. I've sold many captions that originally were rejected—often to the same company a year or two later.

↗ NEVER GIVE UP ON AN IDEA, ESPECIALLY IF YOU LIKE IT! ↗

FINAL THOUGHTS

WRITER'S BLOCK

We've all heard the nightmare scenario. The blank sheet of paper, the unrelenting, blinking cursor against the empty computer screen screaming for words—any words—to be imprinted upon them, while the writer's mind is *blocked* beyond repair.

I hate to burst a venerated, long-standing notion here, but the concept of writer's block is nonsense. My friend and mentor, Eva Shaw, says it better than anyone in her book on ghostwriting: "Writer's block is a hoax perpetuated by unsuccessful writers."   I believe, as she does, that this canard simply provides many a "writer" with the convenient excuse not to sit down at the keyboard and just get down to business.

Not only that, but as greeting card writers, we have absolutely no excuse to fall back on blocked brain cells. First, we jot down ideas for our captions on unintimidating, spiral note paper. Then we type them on a 3x5" index card. Our problem, generally, is to cut down on words because the card gets filled up too fast.

I'll concede there may be periods when nothing you put down on paper seems right. You'll have a perfect punch line, but your outside caption is cumbersome or doesn't lead into the inside line smoothly. You'll find a terrific expression, but you can't seem to match it to an appropriate occasion. Everything you try writing in that short, snappy, funny style comes out awkward, clumsy, flat.

Do you panic? I hope not. When these periods happen to me, I think of them as my "passive creative time." While I might slow down my actual caption writing, I still continue working just the same—checking out card racks, flipping through magazines, listening to conversations for current phrases. I pour through my files—especially the "ideas" and "visual" files. I watch old movies; listen to songs that evoke memories. I take walks. In the summer, I dig in the dirt; when fall comes, I shuffle through leaves.

In other words, I let my senses get creatively re-involved in everything around me. And because I don't believe in writer's block, nor give it credence, I've come to enjoy these passive times; in fact, all too quickly they seem to pass and I find myself, once again, behind the computer screen, writing with renewed purpose, having subtly passed into active mode.

YOUR VERY BEST: WHAT EXACTLY IS THAT?

I know what you're thinking: *Now how can anyone be against sending out only your very best work?* Allow me to throw out the opposite view of this oft-repeated piece of advice, which is "never second guess an editor." This is especially true with greeting card ideas; remember, unlike most other genres, where you send out a single story or article, in a batch of greeting card submissions, you have 11 different concepts to be judged at one time.

In an article I wrote for Oatmeal Studios' newsletter several years ago, I addressed this issue, along with others.

"My solution to this [deciding which ideas are your best work] is, when I have a whole batch of "Really Good Stuff," I never send it all in one envelope. I mix in the ideas I'm particularly excited about with some older, reworked ideas, some ideas that made it to Final Review at one time or another and one or two pieces of copy I know would never sell in a blue moon. Over the years I've discovered that this eclectic mix gives me the best chance for a sale..."

I've found in my own career and in tracking some of my students' successes, that often we really don't know what our very best work is. Sure, *very best*, physically, means no misspellings, no grammatical errors, the standard submission format on 3x5" cards, etc. But our creative "very best?" Many times, I've sent what I considered great copy, only to have it come winging back without even a comment attached.

The reverse has happened as well. I've stuck in an idea at the last minute merely to get to that magic number 11 and you guessed it. That's the one that sold. Also, if you pack all your "very best" into one envelope and they all come back rejected (it happens), where do you go from there? Psychologically it's devastating to have all your best stuff—what you consider to be your best stuff—returned, unsold.

Remember, the freelance submission of your creative work is as much a psychological exercise as a physical one. Mix and match those greeting card ideas—be as open-minded in your selection of ideas to send as you are in the process of creating those ideas—and that open-mindedness will be rewarded with a check.

FIRST SALE SYNDROME

I discovered First Sale Syndrome (FSS) the hard way—I lived through it. Let me set the scene.

You've sent out several batches of ideas with no luck. One day, you open the mailbox and see yet another SASE returned to you. But wait. As you open the envelope and see the familiar stack of 3x5" cards, you also see something out of the ordinary. Instead of the generic slip of paper saying, "Thanks, but no thanks," you see a typewritten letter accompanied by...a check. **A check!** Yes, it's finally happened; you've sold an idea to an editor! Someone out there thought enough of your work to pay for it.

After a few days of euphoria, staring at your check (don't worry—you'll still cash it eventually), rereading the acceptance letter and laughing all over again at the wonderfully witty caption that captivated your editor, you're ready to plunge back into sending out your ideas, only this time with renewed energy and confidence.

I hate to break a bubble here, but you're also a prime candidate for First Sale Syndrome. This insidious condition involves the subtle transformation from *hope* into *expectation*. When you started writing, you hoped to sell and all your efforts were directed to that end. Now that you've sold your first verse, you *expect* to sell, even if you're not consciously aware of it. What you once considered a dream has suddenly become reality and you begin to adjust your sights accordingly. My own experience confirms this. The worst point in my career was not the first year, when I sold only three captions. I was still so thrilled I was actually selling that the "rush" counteracted any negative feelings over the rejections that still poured in.

However, during the second and third year, I was often depressed and, more than once, decided to quit writing greeting cards, even though in that time I sold eight times the amount of material. I wrote captions, absolutely convinced they would sell, only to have them come back, rejected. When five or six envelopes in a row would be returned, my enthusiasm and resolve would plummet. How could I sustain a career when the editors refused to hold up their end of the bargain by buying my ideas?

That's precisely why First Sale Syndrome is so insidious. It attacks right at the time when you're on the threshold of breaking through with regular, consistent sales. You must have a kind of blind faith; if you see your sales are increasing, no matter how slowly or how many rejections come between the acceptances, you are on the right track writing-wise. Your sales will continue to increase and your initial expectations will turn into reality.

I've talked with enough other freelance writers in varied stages of their careers to realize they've all experienced FSS in one form or another. While they may not attach a specific name to it, the experience is a common one. Knowing this creative let-down is a normal part of your career which others have gone through and survived, will hopefully, make it easier to endure when your turn comes around to experience it.

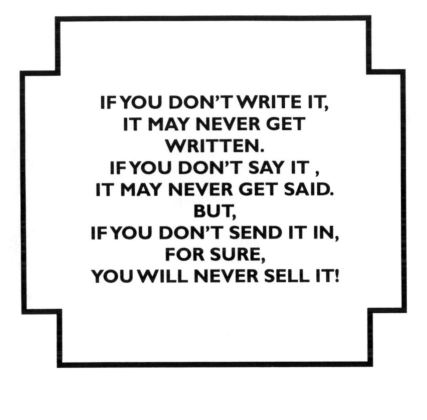

**IF YOU DON'T WRITE IT,
IT MAY NEVER GET
WRITTEN.
IF YOU DON'T SAY IT ,
IT MAY NEVER GET SAID.
BUT,
IF YOU DON'T SEND IT IN,
FOR SURE,
YOU WILL NEVER SELL IT!**

APPENDIX A:
SELECTED CARD COMPANIES

Here are some selected card companies to get you started. Sources to find others are listed in Appendix B.

Amberley Card Company
11510 Goldcoast Drive
Cincinnati, OH 45249-1695
Editor: Dave McPeek

Argus Communications
P.O. Box 9550
Allen, TX 75013-9550
Editor: Amy Craft

Blue Mountain Arts, Inc.
Dept. SML
P.O. Box 1007
Boulder, CO 80306-1007
Contact: Editorial Staff

Comstock Cards
600 So. Rock Blvd, #15
Reno, NV 89502-4115
Manager: David Delacroix
(Note: Uses risqué copy)

DaySpring Cards
P.O. Box 1010
Siloam Springs, AR 72761
Freelance Editor: Ann Woodruff

Kate Harper Designs
P.O. Box 2112
Berkeley, CA 94702

It Takes Two, Inc.
100 Minnesota Ave., Dept. SL
LeSueur, MN 56058
ATTN: Kimberley Rinehart

Laura Leiden Calligraphy Inc.
P.O. Box 141
Watkinsville, GA 30677

Leanin' Tree Publishing Co.
6055 Longbow, Box 9500 West
Boulder, CO 80301
ATTN: Freelance Editors

Oatmeal Studios
Box 138, Dept. SL
Rochester, VT 05767
Editor: Dawn Abraham

Red Farm Studio
1135 Roosevelt Avenue
P.O. Box 347
Pawtucket, RI 02862-0347
Contact: Production Coordinator

Renaissance Greeting Cards
P.O. Box 845
Springvale, ME 04083-0845
Verse Editor: Janice Keefe

SNAFU Designs
Box 16643
St. Paul, MN 55116
Editor: Scott F. Austin

NOTES:

APPENDIX B: SOURCES

Below are some valuable sources you'll want to check out to aid you in caption writing.

Writer's Market (Published Yearly)
F&W Publications
Cincinnati, OH 45207

Greetings etc.
Edgell Publications, Inc.
10 W. Hanover Avenue, Suite 107
Randolph, NJ 07869-4214
Ph: 973/895-3300; Fx: 973-895-7711
e-mail: edgell@edgellmail.com

Greeting Card Association
1200 G Street, N.W., Suite 760
Washington DC 20005
Ph: 202/393-1778; Fax 202/393-0336

Writer's Club University on the Internet
www.writersclub.com

Established in 1998, the WCU offers a wide variety of writing courses, including my 6-week class on greeting card writing, based on my successful "live" course for CCAC-Pittsburgh.

Four additional books in the *Write Well & Sell Series:*

Easy Writing, Easy Money by Mary Jo Rulnick

Mary Jo's experience publishing how-to articles in leading national magazines—including **Disney's** FamilyFun, **Disney's** Games On The Go and **Highlights For Children**—forms the basis for her book on writing the how-to article. Whether your interest is fishing, cooking, coin collecting or gardening—or you've had experience dealing with difficult, stressful situations—Mary Jo's book will lead you through the process of turning this knowledge into a successful how-to article.

Changing Life's Simple Stories Into Sales by Judith Burnett Schneider

Judith Schneider has sold her work to such publications as GRIT Magazine, The Cricket Magazine Group, Children's Better Health Institute Magazines and Cleveland Plain Dealer. With the popularity of the famous *Chicken Soup For the Soul* Books, personal stories have escalated in demand; Judith's many practical exercises, quizzes and bonus tips will guide you toward telling your own story. Her book has been endorsed by former Pittsburgh Steeler, now motivational speaker, **Rocky Bleier**.

Self-Publishing Made Simple by Mary Jo Rulnick & Judith Burnett Schneider

With more publishing houses downsizing and cutting back on titles, self-publishing is a positive alternative.

Authors Rulnick and Schneider share the basic steps designed to propel you on your path to publication. Each step is outlined with directives and examples, answering such questions as How Do I Begin?, Is My Idea Strong Enough? and What Is An Acceptable Format For My Book? If you've ever dreamed of reaping the monetary and personal rewards of seeing your name in print, this book is for you.

Short, Do-Able Writing by Sandra M. Louden (coming in Spring 2000)

If you've enjoyed this book on Greeting Card Writing by Sandra Miller-Louden, you'll also benefit from Short, Do-Able Writing. Sandra, once again, takes you step-by-step through unique writing genres that many people have never considered, including: book reviews, eulogies, greeting cards, fillers, quizzes, reminiscences, lists, and short fiction. With her own column in *Ohio Magazine*, as well as having her fiction chosen **20th** of **7,500** in prestigious **STORY Magazine** competition, Sandra's writing work has appeared in such major publications as *A&E's Biography, CATS, Boys' Life, Yankee, Poet's Market 2000, Pennsylvania Magazine, Writer's Digest, Pittsburgh Tribune-Review, Pittsburgh Post Gazette* and *The Virginian-Pilot & The Ledger-Star* (Norfolk).   You'll catch Sandra's enthusiasm and real love for her profession in a book that's crammed full of both theory and down-to-earth, practical advice.

APPENDIX C: GLOSSARY

For easy reference, I've listed some greeting card-related terms and their definitions.

Caption: The text contained in a greeting card.

Deadline: A definite date by which an assignment must be turned in to an editor.

Freelance: Someone who is paid by what she produces. Freelance contrasts with such employment terms as salaried or hourly, where a regular paycheck is issued and benefits are accrued. Other interchangeable words: *independent contractor* or *work-for-hire.*

Hook: The word, or group of words, that fools a reader to misassociate the caption's meaning by jumping to a conventional conclusion.

Impulse Buy: A product most people don't intend to buy when they enter a store, but once seeing it, decide they must have it.

Line: Any group of cards (generally a number divisible by 4) carrying a central theme or look.

Me-To-You: The most basic, vital core of all greeting card writing reflecting why people buy our product.

Out Of The Sleeve: A card that is no longer active in a company's product line.

Potboiler: Refers to writing that someone—especially a freelancer—does while working on a major project to "keep the financial pot boiling." Potboilers are generally quickly written and take a minimum of research.

Rack Impact: The second-and-a-half each card has to catch the consumer's eye.   A successful rack impact may be achieved through witty text, colorful artwork, stunning photography or a successful melding of these elements.

Spinner: A revolving stand used as a way of displaying greeting cards, generally reserved for a distinct line.   A smaller company that does not produce a large line of cards may also use a spinner to display its products.

Tag Line: A caption for a photo or any other kind of line that introduces a topic. In greeting cards, a tag line (also referred to as "cover headline") is the "throwaway line" that gets the writer into the main text. "Happy Birthday To A Darling Sister" is a tag line.

APPENDIX D:
IT'S ABOUT TIME, BUT...

I hope you've found this book as much fun to read as I had writing it for you. Greeting card writing is all about having fun. As I tell my students, the concept of "fun" is not as flaky a criterion as you might think at first glance. Our text is so short, so immediate, so "in your face" that any attempt at fudging, any breakdown in enthusiasm is immediately apparent.

What initially makes you pick up a greeting card off the rack? Not the words, but the artwork, right? But what makes you **buy** that greeting card? Maybe, in part, the artwork, but more than likely, the words and the emotion behind the words. Does that mean one aspect is more important the other? Of course not. It means they both meld together to form that perfect whole known as a greeting card.

Your contribution as a freelance writer to this product is invaluable. It should please you that your words are found across the country—even across the world. (I saw one of "my" cards in a village in Cornwall, England several years ago.) As I've said before, you probably won't get rich writing captions (although I could name a few people who have), but you'll have a grand time just the same. I can't tell you the number of students who have told me out of all the writing they do, greeting cards remain their favorite.

Questions? Comments? I'm here. Below is information for contacting me. Keep writing. Keep sending in those ideas. All best to you always.

<u>Write me</u>:
Sandra M. Louden
P.O. Box 9701
Pittsburgh, PA 15229-0701
(Please include an SASE for a reply)

<u>Or e-mail me</u>:
FelshamLdy@aol.com